"With simplicity and w
holiness in the life of all
set by a demanding God, but rather the ___
invitation to share in His divine nature. *An Unnatural Beauty* helps us to
see Who is calling us and how we can respond to this call. I recommend
this little book to those who wish for a deeper, more intimate relationship
with God, from which flows a true reflection of His character."

TIMOTHY C. TENNENT, PHD, President
Professor of World Christianity, Asbury Theological Seminary

"My shelves are loaded with books about God and His holiness, but *An
Unnatural Beauty* is unique among them. You won't be bogged down in
theory, rhetoric, and debate. You will discover how to pursue the Holy
One and to reflect the beauty of His holiness to those around you. Simple
profundity and practicality make this little book's weight disproportionate
to its size. Here is the witness of one who has lived in God's presence and
emerged to share what she has learned over an open Bible as she has
gazed upon the holy, holy, holy God."

REV. JOHN KITCHEN, Author and International Pastor

"*An Unnatural Beauty* holds a simple, fundamental reminder: to be holy,
we must die to self. Self, as Esther writes, is 'that part of us that competes
with God.' When we turn from self and worship Jesus, our faces will shine
with His beauty. This beautiful book is filled with not only foundational
truths from Scripture but also relatable stories and rich quotes from
men and women of old whose lives reflected the beauty of Christ. Thank
you, Esther, for this lovely encouragement to forget about ourselves and
concentrate on Jesus so that we can exchange our chaos for His peace,
overflow with His love and joy, and reflect the beauty of His holiness.

REBECCA ENGLISH LAWSON, Owner and operator of GladBooks
Editorial Services, Compiler of *Living the Christ Life: A Collection of
Daily Readings by Classic Deeper-Life Authors*

"Thank you, Esther Lovejoy, for your important reminder that living
a life of holiness is not optional or impossible. *An Unnatural Beauty:
Rediscovering the Beauty of Holiness* is must reading for every Christian
who longs to reflect God's character through all they say and do."

MARLENE BAGNULL, Author, Conference Director Colorado Christian
Writers Conference and Greater Philadelphia Christian Writers Conference

an unnatural
beauty

Rediscovering the beauty of holiness

M. ESTHER LOVEJOY

ST JOSEPH, MISSOURI USA

Cover photo:
Cover design by Tamara Clymer

Printed in the United States of America

Dedication
To four of my greatest blessings:
Debbie, Dan, Bridgette, and Steven

Contents

Foreword

*Y*ou're beautiful!" As a father of two girls, I have said these words in my home many times. Each and every time I have meant them with all of my heart. Sometimes they're said on a special occasion, like when my oldest daughter came out of her room dressed for her first formal. Her beauty took my breath away and immediately had me questioning why I would ever let her out of our house into a world that included teenage boys!

Other times they're spoken as a result of something I see in their character. My youngest daughter's beauty was on full display as she lovingly and carefully crafted a card for a friend who had just lost her grandmother. Often times, however, those words are not spoken because of any event or because of any action but simply because they are true! My girls are beautiful and, as a father, I want to make sure they hear that truth on a daily basis.

I also want them to know this beauty is not tied to the way they look or the way they act. They are beautiful simply because of the way God made each of them. I want them to perceive and fully embrace the reality that true beauty can only be found as a reflection of the beauty of the One who lovingly and perfectly created them.

Why is this so important to me? Because this truth challenges the persuasive message of the world that values appearance above character. Genuine beauty is when our hearts respond to the loving call of God the Father to mirror His holiness in our lives. This is the message of *An Unnatural Beauty*, a message that is desperately needed in a world that is obsessed with the pursuit of beauty at all costs. A world caught up in the outer trappings and temporary fixes we have mistakenly convinced ourselves will make us beautiful. Oftentimes, this comes at the expense of what God defines as truly beautiful.

As a father to girls, I love this message. However, this is not a book whose topic is limited in any way to the development of a healthy view of beauty in a young girl's mind. This is a message sorely needed across every available teaching platform in our churches. Men and women, young and old are invited by God to be holy as He is holy.

As a pastor I have watched the people I serve struggle with this call to holiness. I have seen those who get so caught up in striving for holiness in their own strength that their life becomes a joyless series of rights and wrongs to be balanced against each other. It seems that at the end of the day the final tally always leans the wrong way. I've seen others who simply write off the call to holiness as an impossible command God didn't really mean as they choose to hold up the grace of God as an excuse to live the way they want. The vast majority fall somewhere in the middle, genuinely desiring to be a better reflection of God's holiness but not really understanding what that entails. This is a book for everyone!

Esther has perfectly captured the intricacies of holy living as a response to the invitation of God in our lives. She masterfully introduces and develops the idea of holiness, not as a series of actions, but as a worshipful response to the love of the Father in our lives. We are invited, as a part of God's family, to join Him in holiness. We are not left to our own devices to figure out what that may look like or how we can achieve this, but with God's call comes His provision and enabling to fully display His holiness, His beauty to the world around us.

Drawing from her own personal experiences as well as God's covenant relationship with Israel in the Old Testament, Esther paints a picture of personal holiness that is not an unattainable standard but rather a natural outcome of a life passionately devoted to our relationship with God. Esther weaves stories throughout the book that make tough concepts understandable by connecting them to our everyday lives.

Finally, I have a vantage point that few others have that lends to the credibility of what is written within the pages of this book. Esther is my mother. I have had a front row seat to many of the lessons she has learned in her life and reflects on here. My mother is not perfect. Our life growing up was not perfect. But I have watched my mother gaze unswervingly into the eyes of Jesus, I have watched her reflect His character in the ways she interacts with people, and I have watched her trust Him to bring about good in things that were clearly intended for evil. She has not just written this book; she has lived it. She is not simply the author of *An Unnatural Beauty;* she is the picture of it as well. I pray God uses this book to speak to your life as much as my mother's life has spoken to mine.

Rev. Daniel J. Richter
Pastor, Durham Evangelical Church

Introduction

> "How little people know who think that holiness is dull. When one meets the real thing…it is irresistible." ~C. S. Lewis

*B*eauty is big business. Pick up any women's magazine and immediately you are confronted with ads offering products to get rid of wrinkles, cover gray, and smooth skin tone. There are articles that instruct us how to tighten our tummies, what clothes to wear, what clothes not to wear, what shade of lipstick is now in vogue, and the newest, guaranteed way to take off those extra pounds (do any of these really work?).

God is also serious about beauty and it is "advertised" throughout all of Scripture. In contrast to the beauty advertised in magazines and on television, the beauty of holiness is timeless and unfading, not hindered by age or wrinkles. Sadly, this beauty is considered by many to be an unrealistic and unattainable goal. I want to encourage you that the beauty of holiness is not only real, but possible. The "unnatural beauty" God offers is not a vague Christian ideal, but a wonderful and practical invitation from a holy God.

God loves beauty. Creation is a dramatic display of His ability to speak into existence things of great beauty. His detailed design for the tabernacle also demonstrates His desire for beauty. And He has assured us even our imaginations can't envision the beauty He has prepared for us eternally.

But with all the beauty that has its origins in God, none can compare or equal the beauty of His holiness. It is declared in triplicate by those who worship around His throne. It is the truest and purest essence of who He is, and it is this that He offers to share with us. We are invited to be a display for the beauty of God's holiness—a beauty that has no other source but that of a holy, holy, holy God.

Holiness is a word that has many negative associations. It conjures up images of out-of-date clothes, no makeup, and an endless list of "thou shalt nots." Over the years, we have turned holiness into a *what*—and usually a rather rigid, negative *what* rather than a glorious *Who*.

Sadly, the concept of holiness is often seen as an outdated term no longer relevant to today's Christian culture. The purpose of *An Unnatural Beauty* is to bring scriptural holiness out into the light where it can again be seen as the joyous privilege God offers to His children.

We need to rediscover the scriptural understanding of holiness. We need to find again the joy, freedom, and genuine beauty that come from sharing in God's divine and holy nature. This is not a book of dos and don'ts. Rather, it seeks to challenge us with God's call to holiness and to encourage us with God's enabling to make this real and practical in our lives. I have known women with this unnatural beauty and long to share this exciting possibility with you.

In the pages ahead, we will look at the scriptural call to holiness and what is involved in our response to this call. We will examine the cost of holiness and see that refining and cleansing, though often unpleasant, are simply a means to the end—and the end is worth the cost. We will discover what holiness is by first looking at what it isn't as we examine some traditional views. We will consider the rewards of pursuing the beauty of holiness, and God's means of accomplishing it in our lives. And throughout all the chapters of this book, we will find the One who is the source of all holiness.

We live in a society where the truth of Christianity is often being drowned out by the messages of our culture or simply ignored. To a large degree, people don't want to hear what we have to say. Against that backdrop it becomes imperative that Christ be seen. It's hard to argue against the genuine beauty of holiness when it is seen in the life of a godly woman. This "unnatural beauty" is what needs to be seen in our homes, in the workplace, and in our churches.

The title of this book bears witness to the truth that this beauty can't be achieved through natural means—it can't be achieved through our own efforts or applied for special occasions. It is the supernatural work of a holy God, an inward work that is evidenced outwardly and truly results in an unnatural beauty. Natural beauty fades, despite all the marketing propaganda to the contrary. God offers us an unnatural but very real beauty that is unhindered by time—the beauty of His own holiness.

Chapter One

Call or Command?

"We are called to be holy simply because we're
designed to be holy." ~Gerard Reed

*L*isa became part of our family at the age of fourteen. Her background did nothing to prepare her for life in a parsonage, or for that matter, life in any normal family environment. Lisa's mother was a drug addict and an alcoholic. She had four children—all by different men, none of whom she was married to at the time. Lisa was given the last name O'Brien because all her mother could remember about the man who fathered her was that he was Irish.

Being the oldest put much of the responsibility for the younger children on Lisa's young shoulders. Seldom did they eat a proper meal, and never did they sit down at a table together. Some of Lisa's first words to us were, "I don't ever want to eat another hot dog!"

We had invited Lisa to live with us while her mother was in rehab. When the time of rehab was over, Lisa didn't want to go home, and her mother made it clear she didn't really want her back, so she continued to live with us as a welcomed and loved part of our family.

While our home life was far from perfect, it was still entirely different from anything Lisa had experienced. We had three young children, all had the same last name, and all shared the same father—my husband. We ate meals together, usually at about the same time each day, and while we did have hot dogs occasionally, we didn't have them every night.

Somehow, we needed to find a way to ease Lisa into our family with its structure and rules. Everything was new and different for her, and even though those differences were good, they were still foreign to anything she had known before.

I sensed instantly that to *command* Lisa to live our way—abide by our rules, live by our standards—would prove frustrating for all of us and lead to repeated conflict. To force our way of life on her could hinder our attempt to build a loving and nurturing relationship. So, what should we do? Our approach was to call her to our way of life—to invite her to join in the lifestyle of our family.

For example, I didn't share Lisa's love for heavy metal rock music. In fact, I was strongly opposed to exposing my young children to that style of music. We were still listening to "Itsy, Bitsy Spider"—a far cry from Metallica. To forbid her to listen to her preference in music guaranteed a battle. My solution was to allow her to listen to her music in the privacy of her room, but at a volume that did not impact the rest of the home. Lisa had a tremendous desire to please us, and so it wasn't long before she chose not to listen to heavy metal rock. (I also suspect heavy metal rock on low volume lost a lot of its appeal.)

Our lifestyle is even further removed from God's than Lisa's was from ours. In ourselves, we have nothing in common with God. As Adam's relatives we have inherited a nature contrary to God's that leaves us incapable of participating in His lifestyle. We can be *good* on our own (for a while), but never holy. C. S. Lewis said, "No man knows how bad he is till he has tried very hard to be good."[1] It is equally true no one knows how unholy they are until they have tried very hard to be holy.

Just as we *called* Lisa to join in our family, to participate in being one with us, God calls us to holiness. He invites us to share in His own divine nature as He lovingly adopts us into His family.

First Peter 1:15–16 state, "as he who called you is holy, so be holy in all you do; for it is written, 'Be holy, because I am holy.'" Many see this verse as a command. Personally, I see it as a wonderful invitation—a call to reflect the nature and character of the One who has chosen us to be His. He called us to be His children, and now He calls us to live in a way that reflects His family and His lifestyle.

How sad so many Christians see this as a heavy burden God has placed on us. They see it as an impossible demand that leaves them frustrated and continually aware of their own failures. They see it as rules and requirements that can never be achieved. Sadly, they miss the privilege of a holy God inviting us, as part of His family, to join in His holy lifestyle.

We know very little about God before He created the world. We know little about what He thought or did or said. However, Ephesians 1:4 offers us a rare and wonderful peek into God's heart prior to creation. Paul, through the Holy Spirit, makes it clear that even then, back before time, God was thinking about us, and those thoughts are of tremendous significance. Listen as Paul shares the heart of God: "even as he chose us in him before the foundation of the world, that we should be holy and blameless before him."

These words make us realize how deeply important it is to God that we display the beauty of holiness. This was His plan—this has always been His plan. He has anticipated this since before creation, and all of creation was to be the backdrop for this glorious display.

The importance of something is often in direct proportion to the length of time we've anticipated it. And the length of time we anticipate something can also impact the degree of disappointment we experience if it doesn't come to fruition.

It was on my honeymoon that I first had a great idea for something special for our twenty-fifth anniversary celebration. When you're a new bride, the idea of your twenty-fifth anniversary seems hard to imagine, but nevertheless, I tucked my wonderful idea away for the far-distant anniversary.

But much more quickly than I imagined, our twenty-fifth wedding anniversary arrived. I had thought of my plan off and on during the years, but as it drew closer to the actual day, my anticipation grew. What a wonderful surprise this was going to be for my husband.

Finally, the day arrived. We had doled our children out to various family and friends and had driven to a cute little cottage located on Lake Erie. Everything was perfect…and then the phone rang. Our daughter Debbie had food poisoning and was terribly sick. Being that sick is horrible—being that sick at someone else's house is even worse. We had no choice but to get in the car and bring our daughter back with us.

My plans for our anniversary had not included caring for a daughter who was sick to her stomach. And so, I began to cry—no, I began to sob! My poor husband was stunned by what he saw as an untypical overreaction to the situation. I was usually a very nurturing mother, and so he was baffled by my response to Debbie's need. He couldn't know my disappointment was directly connected to the longevity of my plans for the evening—twenty-five years of anticipating this time together.

It's important to understand if I had just come up with this idea the night before, or even the week before, the disappointment would not have been nearly so great, but I had planned this for twenty-five years!

God has planned for us to be holy since "before the creation of the world." Imagine how important this is to His heart. Imagine His disappointment when we fail to respond to His call to participate in His life—to share in His eternally glorious and beautiful holiness.

We have been invited by God to be part of His family, but with that invitation comes the call to live according to His own nature—and His nature is holy. Peter makes it clear God's own holiness is not only to be our standard, but it's to be our motivation. "As obedient children, do not be conformed to the passions of your former ignorance, but as he who called you is holy, you also be holy in all your conduct, since it is written: 'Be holy, because I am holy'" (1 Peter 1:14–16).

Many of the blunders Lisa committed when she first came to live with us were made out of ignorance. She was still living based on her old lifestyle. I remember one day when she came bouncing down the stairs ready to go to youth group. We had to gently, but firmly, explain to her that a T-shirt advertising a certain brand of beer, no matter how cute it looked on her, was not appropriate for her to wear to church. This was a reminder that she now represented our family, and we felt it probably wasn't wise for a PK (preacher's kid) to wear that particular shirt to church. She had picked it out of ignorance and readily changed when we explained. Her obedience came from a sincere desire to please us.

That same desire is to be our motivation. Peter begins this verse by saying, "As obedient children." Every illustration God uses to help us understand our relationship to Him is one of love, but perhaps the greatest is that of a father and his children. He wants our desire for holiness to be born out of a love for Him and a desire to please Him.

I have a friend who is presently living a very deliberate life of disobedience to God. She tries to defend her choice by saying she still loves the things of the Lord—she loves to read Christian books and talk with me about spiritual things. What I have tried to gently point out to her is that God measures her love for Him in her obedience. The expression of love is validated by a desire to obey.

God is holy, and we're not. It's that simple. God calls us to a lifestyle unfamiliar to us. He calls us to a lifestyle that can only be learned and lived out in His presence. We never would have expected Lisa to learn the rules and standards of our home apart from living with us. We didn't say, "This is how we live, and when you get it right, then we'll claim you as ours." However, the longer she lived with us, the more she became like us. The more she identified with our family, the more she reflected our standards. But most importantly, the more she understood our love for her, the greater her desire to please us and become one with us.

The parallel is obvious. We are called to be holy. It has been God's desire for us since before the creation of the world. The more time we spend in God's presence, the more we desire to be like Him and to reflect His own holy life. Our desire for Lisa was that she reflect our home and our lifestyle. God's desire for us is that we show through our lives that we are the children of a holy God.

God's call to holiness echoes throughout the pages of Scripture. It was His call to Abram. It was His call to the nation of Israel. It was His call to the fledgling church. And it is His call to us today. He invites us, as part of His family, to display a beauty that is not natural to us—the beauty of holiness.

Personal Reflection and Prayer

How does Ephesians 1:4 impact our view of the call to holiness? Note the words *in Him*. What encouragement do these words offer?

Dear Father,

Scripture so clearly reveals Your heart and desire for us as Your children. This has been Your plan since before the creation of the world. This continues to be Your call to us as Your children. And yet, our own efforts fall so short of this. Thank You that Your call includes Your provision. Thank You for the comfort and encouragement of the words *in Him*. Amen.

Chapter Two

May I Ask Who's Calling?

"The natural man…may fear God's power and admire His wisdom, but His holiness he cannot even imagine." ~A.W. Tozer

Our response to a call depends very much on the one who is calling. I remember sending my youngest son out to call the others in for dinner. He came back very disgusted as he reported they hadn't listened to him. I suggested he add the two words: "Mom says!" Immediately the older children stopped playing and came in. They realized this "call" didn't come from their little brother (whom they could easily ignore), but from their mother, and that made all the difference in their response.

I answer the phone very differently when I know it's my husband than I do for a telemarketer. Imagine the telemarketer's surprise if I were to greet him as warmly as I do my husband. (I doubt they get many warm greetings.) I also respond very differently to what a telemarketer has to say or offer. In fact, my response usually is to hang up as soon as possible. I would never do that to my husband. I love to talk to him, and what he has to say is important to me.

The same is true of our call to holiness. We need to have a clear understanding of who is calling. That understanding will have a great impact on our response. This is not the call of our church, nor is it the call of our pastor. It's not the call of our Christian peers to fit in or conform to their standards. It is the call of the holy, holy, holy God.

The definition of holiness is God. It's more than an attribute or a characteristic of God; it is the very essence of His being. Holiness is not just an aspect of God's nature but the sum total of who He is. Everything we know about Him is born out of and swallowed up in His infinite holiness. God is holy. All else that He is flows from His holiness and is consistent with it.

We can never exaggerate the holiness of God. There are no words that are too grand or too glorious. It requires language that expresses itself in superlatives that are free of hyperboles. And, even then, it is still not adequately expressed.

God's holiness is the characteristic continually and eternally declared by those around His throne. The apostle John had a glimpse of this eternal worship service and shares the scene with us. "Day and night they never stop saying, 'Holy, holy, holy is the Lord God Almighty, who was, and is, and is to come'" (Revelation 4:8).

"They never stop saying, 'Holy, holy, holy…'" I was thinking about that one day and wondered how they could keep continually declaring God's holiness. What struck me was that they can't quit. His holiness continually and eternally evokes an involuntary response of awe and worship. To be in His presence is become acutely and immediately and fully aware of His holiness—and at the same time, to become painfully aware of our own lack of holiness.

This was Isaiah's experience. He was given a glimpse of the throne of God and records the same experience as John. Their consistency is simply because they were gazing at the same scene and watching the same eternal acknowledgement of the holiness of God. They both record that the immediately apparent and outstanding aura of the throne of God was the holiness of God—a holiness that evokes continual praise and worship. I suspect we are much more confident in our ability to describe the holiness of God when we've never had a true glimpse of it. For those who haven't experienced it, language seems adequate. They confidently attempt to express the inexpressible. But to truly experience the awesome reality of God's holiness, even for one fleeting moment, makes us keenly aware of the inadequacy and limitation of our vocabulary. In that moment we are struck dumb and later attempts to describe that moment just point out the failure of words. But words are all we have.

In *The Believers* by Janice Holt Giles, the main character Rachel says: "Words don't really explain. They just tell. It's the only way folks have of telling, but it's a poor way sometimes."[2] Never is this truer than when we attempt to convey the holiness of God. Words are a very poor way indeed, but "it's the only way folks have."

We are not just trying to understand and express something greater than we are; we are trying to understand and express something that is beyond our finite ability to grasp, and therefore, to adequately express. Andrew Murray says holy is a word "of unfathomable meaning." It is, in other words, indescribable. That truth in itself is what makes God's holiness a matter of experience rather than expression.

I was living in Wilmore, Kentucky, during the time of the great Asbury Revival. A group of students had banded together to seek God and ask for His presence to fall on their campus, and God graciously said yes. What began as a typical morning chapel, often attended from a sense of duty rather than desire, lasted without interruption day and night for twelve days. You couldn't walk into Hughes Auditorium without an immediate awareness that you were in God's presence. God came to Asbury and where God is, there is the frightening and wonderful sense of His holiness.

Those of us who were privileged to be there sat encompassed and enveloped in the holiness of God. It caused us to weep in repentance at our own lack of holiness, and to bow in awed worship at His indescribable and glorious holiness.

Many people testified to a strong sense of God's presence even as they entered the town of Wilmore. A story is told of a socialite from Chattanooga who came to Asbury to see what was happening. She immediately leaned over and took off her shoes when she entered the college auditorium. I don't think she was a woman who went without shoes in public very often, but it was done with an acute awareness that she was on holy ground.

In more recent years I have read accounts of the Asbury Revival and shared the video account with others. I am always left with a strong sense that words can never adequately express what we experienced. It really is "a poor way sometimes." But even with limited words, there is still a sense of the holiness of God that clings to the relating of this story.

An illustration of this took place in an adult Sunday School class I taught on revival a few years ago. One Sunday I shared the Asbury Revival video. When it was over, I was amazed to watch about forty adults stand up and leave the room without uttering a word. That had never happened before, but there was truly a *holy hush* that hung over the room, and everyone seemed reluctant to break it.

What caused this response? There is only one answer, and that is the presence of a holy God. His presence can never be separated from His holiness. And to experience His presence is to be acutely aware of His holiness.

This holy God is the One who calls us, and that truth makes all the difference. We can argue with church rules, find fault with the expectation of others, disagree with our pastor, but holiness isn't their call. It is the call of a holy God extending a remarkable invitation for us to share in His holiness.

When sharing about the uniqueness of Christianity, Ravi Zacharias said, "It's a life of perfection that reaches out to the flawed."[3] It's a holy God extending an invitation to flawed and sinful humans. And what's more remarkable is that the invitation includes a call to share in His perfection—His divine nature and holiness.

That is an overwhelming invitation, but the good news is that we are called by a God who offers to do the work for us. "The one who calls you is faithful; and he will do it" (1 Thessalonians 5:24). I love these words, and the context of them makes it clear this is in reference to our sanctification—our holiness. The earlier part of this verse spells it out clearly. "May the God himself, the God of peace, sanctify you through and through. May your whole spirit, soul and body be kept blameless at the coming of our Lord Jesus Christ" (1 Thessalonians 5:23).

What a picture of God's willingness to get involved. God is not calling us from a distance, urging us to do our best at all of this. God understands completely that He has called us to something unnatural, and He offers to do supernaturally what we can't do naturally. (If you doubt the truth of this, just try to be holy on your own for a while.) But God is willing to do for us what we cannot do for ourselves. What a blessing! What a relief!

This verse also gives us a clear indication that God intends to see this work through to the end. Philippians 1:6 assures us "he who began a good work in you will carry it on to completion." God is committed to this. He is in this for the long haul.

I knew a woman who loved crafts. The only problem was that she always found her next must-do project before she had finished the present one. The result was a closet full of unfinished craft projects. She was a great starter, but not a great finisher. God has assured us He won't give up or quit.

I find this very humbling and very encouraging. I can't, but He can! He calls and He enables. A few years ago in an acknowledgment of my inability to produce the beauty of holiness in my own life, I wrote these words:

I am living proof that a deep desire for holiness is not enough, that good intentions are not enough, that a determined will and valiant efforts are not enough. Lord, make me living proof that this is Your work and Yours alone for Your glory. Amen.

My intentions were good, and, oh, how I tried, but the results were a "new and improved" me that never lasted long.

An old hymn written by Dr. A. B. Simpson expresses so well what many of us have experienced:

"I'm weary of sinning and stumbling,
Repenting and falling again;
I'm tired of resolving and striving,
And finding the struggle so vain.
I long for an arm to uphold me,
A will that is stronger than mine;
A Saviour to cleanse me and fill me,
And keep me by power divine."[4]

The good news is that there is an arm to uphold us; there is a will stronger than ours; and there is a Savior willing to cleanse, and fill, and keep us as a glorious display of the beauty of holiness.

Remember, the One who calls you is faithful, and He will do it. He must do it. Part of the road to holiness always includes a cross—death to self—and who can crucify themselves? God chose a death that cannot be self-inflicted.

First Thessalonians 5:23 reveals something else about the

One who calls us to holiness. Look at these words: "through and through…your whole spirit, soul and body." They leave us with no doubt God is not only committed to complete His work in us, but He also intends it to be thorough—a complete makeover.

Most of us love the story of Esther in the Bible. Here was a young Jewish girl who was suddenly thrust into a world of opulence and power. She was one of many girls who would be on display as a candidate for the role of queen. Esther knew the day was coming when she would be called into the king's presence, and it would take more than her own natural beauty to impress the king. The competition was fierce, and the king's demands were nothing short of perfection, but the good news was that the king himself would provide everything she needed to meet those standards. No one expected Esther to have what she needed to enter the king's presence. It was supplied by the king.

God doesn't expect us to have what we need to attain the beauty of holiness. Our own natural beauty—our good characteristics and qualities—aren't enough. But the good news is that the King Himself has made provision.

There is a wonderful example of God's provision in Ezekiel. The prophet saw a revelation of the glory of God and immediately fell facedown. God's instructions to Ezekiel were to stand up on his feet so God could speak to him. I suspect after a glimpse of the glory of God, standing up was not something Ezekiel was capable of at the time. I love the next words. "And as he spoke, the Spirit came into me and raised me to my feet" (Ezekiel 2:2). God's call included God's provision and enabling.

It's important to know it is God Himself who calls us to holiness. And it is God Himself who offers us full provision and His own enabling to respond to that call. The One who calls us is faithful, and He will accomplish what we cannot.

Personal Reflection and Prayer

How important is it that we recognize who's calling us? What difference does that make? Read Psalm 99:9 and take time to prayerfully consider the awesome holiness of the One who calls us.

How do we find encouragement in the story of Esther?

Dear Father,

The beauty of holiness is Yours and Yours alone. The more we see it in You, the more we are brought to our knees in awe and worship, and the more we are aware of our own unholiness. This truly is a beauty that is not natural to us. Thank you that Your call to us includes Your full provision. Thank you for the assurance that "the one who calls you is faithful, and he will do it." We rest in that. Amen.

Chapter Three

Grandma's Bow

"Holiness is not a series of do's and don'ts, but
conformity to the character of God." ~Jerry Bridges

An old joke asks, "How do you make a statue of an elephant?"
The ridiculous answer is that you get a piece of marble and
cut away everything that doesn't look like an elephant. I've never
attempted to make an elephant statue, but I'm pretty sure if I were
to try that approach, the result would not even closely resemble an
elephant.

However, it's said that when Michelangelo looked at a huge piece
of marble, he was able to already envision the statue of David. He
truly did have to just cut away everything that hindered the true
beauty of his famous statue of David from being seen.

Sometimes it really is helpful to peel away all that something
isn't to find a more accurate view of what it is. That's true of
holiness. We catch a clearer glimpse of what it is by first chipping
away at what it isn't.

There are many misconceptions about holiness. There are many things called holiness that aren't. It will be helpful to clear these away so we can see the beauty of what remains.

One day my aunts were looking through an old photo album and found a picture of my grandmother on her wedding day. It was a beautiful picture of Grandma, but what immediately caught their attention was the bow on her hat. It was quite a bow—not one that sat modestly on the side of the brim, but one that was front and center, dominating the hat and the wearer. As part of a strict *holiness* denomination, my aunts were stunned (and amused) by this apparent display of extravagance.

When they commented about the bow to my grandmother, her immediate and emphatic response was, "Well, at least it wasn't a feather!" Apparently, a bow, no matter how large and fancy, was still acceptable on the hat of Christian woman of her day, but a feather crossed some invisible "thou shalt not" line.

Calvin Miller states, "For generations much of the Christian church has foolishly sought to arrive at holiness by code."[5] And that code has often been the difference between a bow and a feather. Just as a grocery list is a far cry from a wonderfully prepared feast, a list of dos and don'ts is a far cry from the reality of genuine holiness.

I've been reading in Leviticus and have been struck by God's continual reminder that He alone could make Israel holy. There, among all the rules and regulations that were to govern their lives, God repeatedly says, "I am the LORD, who makes you holy." They would never arrive at holiness simply by obeying the rules.

So, the first big chunk of *non-holiness* that needs to be removed is the legalism of rules and regulations. God is not legalistic. He's holy, and He doesn't call us to legalism, but to holiness. Sadly, we are often more comfortable with rules than with righteousness, but no matter how many rules we make, God continues to hold out a higher standard—His holiness.

Merriam-Webster Dictionary defines legalism as, "strict, literal, or excessive conformity to the law or to a religious or moral code." The Pharisees were a perfect example of this definition. Never was there a more list-driven, self-righteous group than the Pharisees, but Christ made it clear they had sadly and profoundly missed the mark. He said everything they did was done for men to see, and that brings us to our second *non-holiness* chunk that needs to be cleared away.

Even for those who are free from the idea that holiness is just Christian rules, there is still the risk of seeing it as a matter of behavior. If we can just be good! We are free from the outward regulations that are mistaken for holiness but substitute our own effort to be good instead. But holiness is not about becoming better people. We can make ourselves better. It's not about being good. We can be good. It's about being holy, and our best behavior can't produce holiness. That is a work that can only be done by a holy God.

The only thing our good behavior can produce is self-righteousness, and God describes self-righteousness in very graphic terms that are a far cry from the beauty of holiness. He declares our righteousness to be like "filthy rags" (Isaiah 64:6) to be discarded and of no worth.

The beauty of holiness is not about our behavior, neither is it about our outward appearance. It's far more profound than the difference between a feather and a bow. As a young pastor's wife, I struggled with how I should look. Were pierced ears okay? Should I or shouldn't I wear nail polish? How should I dress? Were shorts appropriate on a warm day for the Sunday School picnic?

These questions seem silly now, but at that time they were motivated by a very sincere desire to find out what pleased God, and, I'm sure, also by the desire as a young pastor's wife to please people. Sadly, spirituality is often judged by outward appearance. Our outward appearance is important, but not a measure of our holiness. I live in a part of the country where many people dress plain. It is just as possible to be proud of a plain look as it is a more glamorous appearance.

God used the tabernacle to teach me an important lesson. The Old Testament tabernacle was a place of great beauty with intricately woven curtains and furnishings of gold—beauty designed by God. But what set the tabernacle apart was not the outward beauty, impressive as that was, but the presence of a holy God.

It's there I found my answer. While God may look on the heart, people still look at the outward appearance, so it was okay for that outward appearance to be attractive. But what needed to be the real attraction in my life was the beauty of holiness displayed by the presence of an indwelling God. He still needs to be the main attraction.

I remember attending a conference on prayer a few years ago. A young woman came up to the microphone dressed in a way that seemed inappropriate to me. As she began speaking, I wondered, "Where did they ever find her? She doesn't seem a very good choice to introduce the speaker."

It wasn't long before I realized she wasn't introducing the speaker; she was the speaker! Fortunately, I didn't let her appearance keep me from listening, and what I heard were words that came from a heart devoted to God. She spoke on prayer from her own joyous experiences of communicating with the Almighty. I was deeply moved by what she shared, and more than slightly rebuked for making an assumption based on her outward appearance.

A P.S. to this story is that she came from a part of the country where her dress was very stylish. I came from a part of the country that hadn't quite caught up yet. Outward appearance is important, but, whether plain or fancy, it is not an indicator of holiness.

Another misconception about holiness is that it's optional or for a select few. God's repeated plea for the nation of Israel to be holy included all of them, not just Moses and the priests. Leviticus 19:2 makes this clear. God instructs Moses to speak to the entire assembly of Israel and say to them: "Be holy because I, the LORD your God, am holy." God didn't have Moses gather together a few of the Israelite elite. This was for all of His people. It still is!

As we remove the things that aren't holiness, another big chunk is a lie from the enemy that this is an unattainable ideal. We may understand holiness is not legalism; it's not man-made rules and regulations. There is an equal risk of seeing it as a mere sentimentality—an ideal to aim toward, but not one that is realistic or can ever be achieved. That takes holiness from the absolute of rigid rules to an unrealistic goal.

Andrew Murray makes a clear argument to the contrary. His biographer shares, "Andrew warned of the danger in thinking that such experiences are exceptional and that holiness is optional. He said that the possibility argues its necessity. That it is attainable shows that it is indispensable."[6]

Absolute holiness is God's alone, but the beauty of holiness is attainable. God doesn't call us to something that can never be achieved to frustrate or discourage us. He holds before us a glorious invitation to share in His own divine nature—a privilege offered to us as His children.

Usually, if we know a goal can never be reached, we give up trying. Satan knows the power and influence of the beauty of holiness displayed in the lives of God's children. He would love for us to believe that it is an idealistic, unattainable goal.

When we have chipped away all that holiness is not, what is left is this glorious truth: Holiness is not a what, but a Who! It's not how we behave, what we think, how we react or respond to life and the people around us. It's not the difference between a bow and a feather. It's something so much more amazing and profound. It's God! It's His divine life being glimpsed in our finite lives here on Earth.

That truth brings with it great freedom. The beauty of holiness doesn't depend on us. We can quit striving only to be met with defeat. It also brings such a sense of awe. God is willing to allow His holy and divine nature to be seen in us—in our daily life, in our circumstances, and in our relationships.

Peter makes this perfectly clear when he shares God has made it possible for us to "participate in the divine nature" (2 Peter 1:4). God is willing to allow the beauty of His holiness to be displayed in us. It's not a beauty that is natural to us, but it is a beauty that is available to us. What an amazing privilege!

Personal Reflection and Prayer

What have been some of your own misconceptions of holiness? How have these impacted you? What difference does it make to understand that holiness is not a what but a Who?

Dear Father,

Forgive us for our ideas about holiness that fall so far short of the true beauty of holiness. Forgive us for worrying about bows and feathers. Free us from the bondage of man's ideas of holiness so we can experience the true beauty of holiness that is found in You and You alone. Amen.

Chapter Four

Doing What Comes Naturally

"It's not by looking at sin that we see it for what
it is, but by looking at the love of God and His
pure holiness." ~Amy Carmichael

Anti-aging creams are popular because wrinkles are not. My little granddaughter was riding with her father when she suddenly declared, "Grandma is old!" He proved his worth as a son when he immediately responded, "Your grandma is not old! Why did you say that?" Her response of "because her face has some little cracks" was one that resulted in much laughter followed by an immediate phone call to me—the cracked-faced grandmother. "Cracks" come with age, and as a result, there is a vast billion-dollar industry marketing products promising to fix those cracks and defy what comes naturally.

This same granddaughter was styling my hair one day and said, "Grandma, you don't have very much gray." Just as I was beginning to get a little puffed up from that remark, she continued with, "for your age." Those annoying gray hairs are more evidence we won't stay young forever. Some gray earlier than others; however, I am one of those blessed with not much gray hair "for my age"—just ask my granddaughter.

Just as wrinkles and gray hair are natural enemies of our youthful appearance, there are also natural enemies to the beauty of holiness. However, they don't wait to appear at old age but are evident very early on in our lives.

The first of these is sin. We are born with inherited sin (thank you, Adam!), but it isn't long until we each prove if Adam hadn't sinned, we would have. God gave us the freedom to make wrong choices—to choose our way over His—and we have all exercised that freedom at one time or another. Those of us who have raised children know this sinful nature reveals itself at a very early age.

One of my little ones had asked for some cheese crackers, a favorite snack of his. It was too close to dinner and he had recently had a snack, so I said no. A few minutes later, I met this same little guy coming down the steps with a mouth full of cheese crackers. Realizing he had been caught, his immediate response was, "God said I could have some cheese crackers. Wasn't that nice of Him?" I reminded him God had also said he was to obey his mother.

While that's a cute story, it still displays our innate desire to have our own way and our willingness to shift the blame to someone else. We all bear a remarkable family resemblance to Adam.

However, Adam's sin was greater than just a simple act of disobedience. Adam and Eve doubted the very words of God. The first words we hear the serpent (Satan) say are, "Did God really say?" (Genesis 3:1). His dart was aimed at their confidence in the absolute truth of God's words—in God's honesty. He adds to those doubts by assuring them that, despite what God had said, "You will not certainly die" (Genesis 3:4).

Adam and Eve also doubted the heart of God. They began to suspect God was withholding something good from them. Scripture says Eve saw the fruit was "good for food and pleasing to the eye" (Genesis 3:6). I'm sure there was other fruit in the Garden that also qualified as "good for food and pleasing to the eye," but this particular fruit had one other thing going for it. The serpent assured them this forbidden fruit was "desirable for gaining wisdom."

Imagine the thought process of Adam and Eve at this point. Nudged on by the tempter, they suddenly became suspicious of God's heart and motive. Here was this beautiful, desirable fruit that offered them wisdom beyond their own. Why would God be so mean-spirited as to keep them from eating something that would make them more like Him? What kind of a loving God would keep them from this pleasure? And so, Adam and Eve ate the forbidden fruit in an act that clearly demonstrated they also doubted the authority of God. What right did He have to tell them they couldn't enjoy this fruit? What right did He have to keep them from the enjoyment of something this enticing?

I imagine the fruit really was delicious, maybe more delicious than anything they had tasted before, but, oh, the aftertaste it left in their mouths as they suddenly felt exposed and naked. Satan had coated his lies with enough truth to make them sound logical and convincing—he was partly right. They now did know the difference between good and evil, but it was not the gain that had been promised. Instead, in that moment, they experienced an eternal loss still felt by each of us today.

Sin! It's our natural state and the enemy of holiness. Our lives bear continual proof that sinning against God comes far more naturally than living a holy life. This struggle is not a new one and we hear the echo of this in Paul's words from Romans 7:18. "For I know that good itself does not dwell in me, that is, in my sinful nature. For I have the desire to do what is good, but I cannot carry it out." We hear the anguish of this struggle when he declares in verse 24, "What a wretched man I am!"

Sin is a problem, and it is especially a problem in our relationship with a holy God. The root of sin hasn't changed since the Garden of Eden. It still finds its source in doubting God's truth, questioning His heart or motive, and rebelling against His absolute authority.

An old Greek hymn expresses the sin-problem like this:

My God, shall sin its power maintain
And in my soul defiant live!
'Tis not enough that Thou forgive,
The cross must rise and self be slain.[7]

"The cross must rise and self be slain." In those words we find the second natural thing that stands opposed to the beauty of holiness—self.

When Adam and Eve sinned, they immediately became aware of themselves. They had made a choice to satisfy their own self-centered desires, and in doing so, they lost their sense of identity that came from being God's and found who they were apart from that relationship. They felt naked. They had always been naked, but now they saw themselves exposed in their sinfulness and loss of innocence. They made a choice to honor self instead of God, and without the covering of God's presence, they saw themselves as they truly were.

Self is the driving force behind sin. It is where sin originates. Years ago, there was a television show starring a comedian named Flip Wilson. In his comedic routines he would often use the line, "The devil made me do it." That line lasted far longer than the television show and was used to lightly excuse a lot of inappropriate behavior. How convenient to have someone else to blame. It relieves us of responsibility for our own choices and actions and portrays us as helpless victims of the devil.

That would be nice if it were true. However, the truth is, the devil can't make us do anything. Sin begins with us—with our *self*. My little guy wanted cheese crackers and that desire led to his disobedience. We see that same process played out in our own lives in far more serious ways.

Satan didn't make Adam and Eve eat that fruit. He didn't use physical force or threaten them if they didn't. He just simply appealed to that part of Adam and Eve called *self*—that part of all of us where sin begins.

Self is a word we hear frequently in our culture. We're encouraged to have good self-esteem, to do things that bring self-gratification, to work hard to become self-sufficient, and to find self-fulfillment. We're urged to work at our self-confidence, our self-awareness, and our self-image. There's even a magazine simply titled *Self*. And so, we need to begin by understanding what we mean by *self*.

Merriam-Webster defines self as "an individual's typical character or behavior." That doesn't sound too bad. It's simply who we are. God loves who we are. He created us, and just as we see such variety in nature, we see variety in human nature, and I think that must delight the heart of our Creator.

So then, why does the Greek hymn writer quoted above declare self needs to be slain? Why must there be a death to something that pleases the heart of God? The word *self* when used in this sense has a different meaning than *Merriam-Webster* gives. It is, simply put, that part of us that competes with God—that part of us that wants to claim rights that are God's alone.

We see the evidence of self in Adam and Eve when they doubted God's words, when they didn't trust His heart, and when they questioned His authority. And we see it often in our own lives when we struggle to submit to God's instructions or guidance.

Self loves to rise up and defend its rights and position. Self loves to demand its own way and rely on its own judgment. Self is the antithesis of Proverbs 3:5, which warns us to not depend on our own understanding. Self feels very confident leaning hard on its own ideas of what is best and right. Self loves to listen to those whispers, "Did God really say?"

Self is not only the part of us that competes with God's authority, it's also that part of us that competes with God's glory. We don't mind serving, but we want others to notice. We don't mind giving, but we want people to acknowledge our gifts. We love the pats on the back, the voices admiring our work and our commitment.

When my son was little, he bought his sister a doll for Christmas with his own money. Other years we had given him money to buy gifts, but that year he had saved his allowance and unselfishly wanted to use it for his sister. He really enjoyed picking out just the right doll and proudly handing the clerk his very own money. Debbie was thrilled with the doll, but after a few days seemed to have lost interest. When asked about it she said, "If I hear he spent his own money on this doll one more time, I'm going to scream."

The truth behind that story was that even though my son had used his allowance—his "own money," for that gift—it was still money that had come from us. He wouldn't have had the money if it hadn't been given to him.

We have been given so much by God. Our very life comes from Him. Our gifts and abilities, our talents and strengths all come from Him. Paul reminds us in 1 Corinthians 7:7 that "each has his own gift from God." Those gifts are ours to use for the glory of God, but we often display that same characteristic as my son. We don't mind being unselfish as long as someone notices. We want our giving to be seen and appreciated. Self loves to claim the glory that belongs to God alone. It loves to point to the gift instead of the Giver.

As a young pastor's wife, I began to be asked frequently to speak. I loved these opportunities to talk about God (I still do!), but I also loved the responses. I loved the positive comments, the encouraging words, and the praise. And I hated that I loved them.

I remember crying out to the Lord in repentance (again!) after enjoying the comments and pats on the back after a time of speaking. I finally told the Lord I didn't want to speak again until I could keep self from claiming glory and praise that should be His alone.

I didn't get asked to speak again for a year. Before, there had been frequent invitations; now there were none. And I knew why. There was a part of me that was competing with God for glory that was rightfully His. Self!

This wasn't a small thing. This wasn't just an area where I needed an attitude adjustment. This was self rising up to claim something that was God's alone. In Isaiah 48:11 God makes this very clear when He says, "I will not yield my glory to another." Add to that the reminder in 1 Corinthians 10:31 that whatever we do, we are to "do it all for the glory of God."

God isn't being selfish here. He's being right! God wanted to be seen in my life, and that couldn't happen if I were taking credit and glory for His work through me. It may have been my "allowance," but it had come from Him. The only remedy was that "The cross must rise and self be slain."[8]

Self also loves to rely on its own goodness. God says, "I alone am holy," and self responds by pointing out we really do have some good qualities—we aren't all that bad. One of the greatest hindrances to holiness is the sense of our own goodness—our self-righteousness. We may be able, by virtue of our own goodness, to stay within the moral code of the church, but we will, by hindrance of that same goodness, fall far short of God's call to holy living. The fact is, we have no personal holiness. It's either His or it's a fraud.

And, above all, self does not want to die! "Self's great, eternal ambition is to escape the cross and sneak back on the throne."[9] However, our rightful place is the cross so a holy God can reign on the throne of our life. The following poem shares my own struggle with this:

My Choice

I've sensed the call of God today to walk with Him a closer way,

A way not understood by some, and so I pause, yet He says, "Come."

He bids me hear no other voice, to make His way my only choice,

But I am comfortable right here with friends and things that I hold dear.

His path ahead seems filled with loss; I see the shadow of the cross,

And though the end I cannot see, I fear this path means death for me!

And self would choose a brighter way, still, "Follow me," I hear Him say,

"The path you dread is one I've trod; the end you cannot see is God."

And so I follow, fearful, yes, but knowing that His way is best

I choose the path to Calvary, for death to self means Christ to me.

"Death to self" may sound like archaic or antiquated theology. Even the teachings of the Church today often avoid this and focus on using Christ to find our true selves and our full sense of identity. Malcolm Muggeridge declares, "It is only through the cross that we come to the Resurrection."[10] Our true sense of identity must come from identifying with a crucified Savior so we can then share in His triumphant, risen life and allow His beauty to be seen in us.

We may accept that God is big and we are small, but it's not until we fall before Him fully aware He is all and we are nothing that we finally see a great and liberating truth. To be free from the unrelenting, exhausting pressure of trying to be something and to rest in Him as the great All-in-all is to finally find peace.

"May Christ be seen in me" wrote the songwriter.[11] It's only as Christ is seen in us that we can display the beauty of holiness. Christ alone led a sinless, selfless life. Christ alone is holy. And Christ alone can reveal the beauty of holiness if we will get out of the way and allow Him to be seen.

Personal Reflection and Prayer

We're usually very aware of areas of sin in our lives, but often don't recognize areas of self quite as easily. How does Jeremiah 17:9 confirm this? Now read Jeremiah 17:10 and ask the Lord to search your heart and mind and show you areas hindering you from experiencing the beauty of holiness.

Dear Holy God,

There are things natural to me that hinder the unnatural beauty of Your holiness from being seen in my life. I add my voice to David's plea, "Search me, O God, and know my heart" (Psalm 139:23). I love that you don't reveal those areas of sin or self to condemn, but to cleanse. Amen.

Chapter Five

God Alone

"We have as much of holiness as we have
of God." ~Andrew Murray

The Old Testament relates the story of the love relationship between God and His chosen people, the nation of Israel. It's the story of God's perfect and unfailing love and Israel's struggle to love God alone. It's the story of faithfulness on God's part and repeated unfaithfulness on Israel's part.

As Israel began their journey out of slavery to the land promised to them by God, Moses retreated to Mount Sinai for specific instructions as to how they were to live. In those intimate days in God's presence, Moses received the core values that were to govern them—the Ten Commandments. God began by instructing Israel about their relationship with Him. They were forbidden to have any other gods; they were not to make any images to worship. It's clear this was to be an exclusive relationship. He alone was to be their God. He alone was to be worshipped.

Yet even while Moses was experiencing this amazing encounter with God, while he was learning the instructions God had for His people, the Israelites were breaking the first two of these commandments. They made and were worshipping a golden calf—an idol.

It was while visiting Africa that I saw my first idol. Walking along a dusty road in a small village in Mali, we came across a mound of dirt with rocks and sticks randomly protruding from it. I was told by the missionaries this was one of the gods of this particular village. I experienced so many emotions as I stood looking at this heap of dirt. This wasn't even impressive looking. It wasn't fearsome or beautiful. It was just an ordinary pile of dirt, rocks, and sticks. And yet it was feared and worshipped by the people in this remote village in Africa. It was their god.

My experience while visiting China was very different. There I saw idols that were things of great beauty. They were in ornate temples with lavish displays of gold and vibrant fabrics surrounding them. They were impressive and stunningly beautiful, but, in essence, they were no different than that pile of dirt in the village in Africa.

God declares through the prophet Isaiah, "there is no God apart from me" (Isaiah 45:21). It doesn't matter if it's dirt and stones or beautifully crafted gold, it isn't God. In fact, in an earlier chapter in Isaiah, God points out the obvious irony of idols. A carpenter takes great pains to carve an idol from a piece of wood but then uses the same wood to cook his food and keep him warm. He is worshipping something he himself created rather than the Creator.

God's insistence to the nation of Israel that He alone was to be their God—He alone was to be worshipped—wasn't prompted by an ego trip on God's part. It was prompted by the absolute reality there simply wasn't any other choice. He alone was God! To bow to any other god, no matter how impressive or beautiful, was to bow before nothing. There was no other God—no other being or thing worthy of worship.

One of God's main purposes for Israel was that they were to display this truth to other godless nations. They were to reveal He alone was God, He alone was worthy to be worshipped, and He alone was holy. Israel was to be a missionary nation that bore witness to all the nations around them that their God was great and holy and the only God. The nations around Israel had a variety of images of their gods. Israel was to be God's "image"—visible proof of the only true God. God was to be revealed through them as a nation.

This is stated so clearly in Ezekiel 36:23. Listen to God's words to Israel: "I will show the holiness of my great name, which has been profaned among the nations, the name you have profaned among them. Then the nations will know that I am the LORD, declares the Sovereign LORD, when I am proved holy *through you* before their eyes" (emphasis added).

God didn't ask Israel to go to other nations and tell them about Him. He didn't ask them to send proclamations to other lands declaring their God to be the only true God. He asked them to be living proof through their lives of who He was and of His holiness. God says He longed to show Himself holy through them. Over and over again He stressed it was His holiness that was to shine through Israel. They were to be displaying to the nations around them that unnatural beauty that was God's alone.

This call of God found in the Old Testament is a theme that runs throughout Scripture and is as relevant to us today as it was to the nation of Israel. God still longs to make Himself known to people. He still longs to find those who will be a display of His holiness. We are surrounded by people who need to know He alone is the holy, holy, holy God. He has chosen us just as surely as He chose the nation of Israel as a display of that truth. And it is the beauty of holiness that reveals that message more powerfully than words.

We don't have a pile of dirt we call god or ornately fashioned gold images, but "God alone" applies as certainly to us as it did to the nation of Israel. We are just as prone to find other things to worship as Israel was to make a golden calf. We live in a culture that worships so many other things apart from God. He has called us to be today's Israel—to display the beauty of His holiness to those around us so they will see it is God alone who is worthy of worship.

This truth seems so elementary, so basic, that there's the temptation to nod in agreement and skim over this part. But it's the most fundamental element of the beauty of holiness. It is the one and only God who is holy, and He alone can display His holiness through us in our daily lives.

The Pharisees were hoping to trick Jesus when they asked Him the question, "Teacher, which is the greatest commandment of the Law?" He responded with these words: "Love the Lord your God with all your heart and with all your soul and with all your mind." And then in case there was any doubt in their minds, He emphasized, "This is the first and greatest commandment" (Matthew 22:36–38).

What a description of the love God desires from us. It's a passionate, consuming love that allows no room for any other god. Does that sound familiar? We're right back to the first commandments given to Israel. No other God but God alone is to have our love and worship. Oswald Chambers reminds us, "This abandon to the love of Christ is the one thing that bears fruit in the life, and it will always leave the impression of the holiness and power of God, never of our personal holiness."[12]

It is this love, this exclusive and passionate love, that produces the beauty of holiness. It is this basis for our relationship that safeguards us from reducing holiness to a strict standard of behavior or a set of rules, though we are often more comfortable with rules than with righteousness. But God was calling Israel to a love relationship, and they seemed to miss that truth over and over again. In fact, one of God's very descriptive ways of describing Israel's unfaithfulness was to call them a prostitute. Those are pretty strong words, but they convey the seriousness of God's call to an exclusive love relationship with Israel—and with us.

Israel was to be a holy people. They were to be a display of the holiness of their God so that it would attract other nations who had only piles of dirt or worthless idols of gold. And so it is for us. The beauty of holiness is our best witness. There is no greater resource we have to allow others to see the reality and wonder of our God. It is more powerful than the most masterful argument, more convincing than any carefully crafted rhetoric.

Listen again to these words from Ezekiel 36:23. "Then the nations will know that I am the LORD, declares the Sovereign LORD, when I am proved holy through you before their eyes."

God has desired since the beginning of time to reveal Himself to the world. First there was creation, which bore witness to the greatness of God. The psalmist reminds us the very heavens declare God's glory (Psalm 19:1). Everything in nature is a testimony to a brilliant, unfathomable mind capable of thoughts so far beyond our own that there is still much about nature that remains a mystery even to the greatest scientific minds.

God wasn't just the mind behind all of this. He was the power that spoke it all into being. There is so much evidence in nature it's hard to imagine it can be ignored, but there are many who will adhere to illogical explanations rather than acknowledge the evidence of God seen all around us.

Whether you look big (at the universe) or small (at an atom), you are confronted with a perfection of design that could never have happened by chance. Recently I read a book that discussed the structure of RNA and DNA. There was a lot I didn't understand in my reading, but one thing was clear—their staggering complexities point undeniably to a Creator. In fact, the evidence was so undeniable the famous atheist and author of *There Is No God*, Antony Flew, had to write a second book, *There Is a God*. God is clearly seen in what He has made.

But God also chose a more personal way to reveal Himself. He formed a nation from a single man and his barren wife—Abraham and Sarah. It was His purpose to use this nation as a mighty display of His love and power and to be revealed through them as a holy God. We've already seen how repeatedly they failed at this important calling. God asked them to stand apart from the other nations so He could be seen. Instead, they followed the ways of the nations around them and absorbed not only much of their culture, but also their gods.

God then revealed Himself in a deeply personal and amazing way through His own Son. I never tire of the Christmas story. It was my privilege for many years to plan our Christmas Eve Services. Each year I was awed by this timeless story of God's love displayed in a tiny baby—God's own Son. Jesus Himself stated His purpose was to reveal the Father. He did that through His life, and through His death. How could such a dramatic revelation of God and His love be ignored? And yet it has been.

First creation, then a nation, then God's own Son…and now us! When Jesus returned to heaven, He made it clear it was now our responsibility to make Him known to those around us. What a privilege. What a responsibility.

We live in a frightening day and age. More and more the ability to speak freely about the things of God is being limited. Even where we are allowed to speak, many are tired of our words. They've heard this all before and find it dull and meaningless. Never has there been a greater need for lives through which God can display the beauty and attractiveness of His great holiness. And it begins with an exclusive and passionate love relationship with the living

God. You can live a life bound by rules that are mistaken for holiness, but you will never display a holy God through rules. You can carefully obey the teachings of your church and some may be impressed, but they won't see God. But love God alone with a deep and passionate love and it will begin to show. It will always show.

Ruth Graham, who understood (and lived) this truth, shared this insight: "Do you delight yourself in the Lord, as we are told in Psalm 37:4: 'Indulge yourself with delight in the Lord.' If you enjoy God, you will enjoy prayer and you will enjoy your Bible study. And it will show. You can't hide it."[13]

I love that wording of Psalm 37:4: "Indulge yourself with delight in the Lord." You can never achieve the beauty of holiness—that unnatural beauty—apart from loving God alone with all of your heart, soul, and mind. It will show!

Elizabeth Jackson was an amazing woman who loved all of us who called Christie Dorm our home while attending Nyack College. As Dean of Women she put up with our giggling (often long after curfew), ignored the smell of popcorn (which we were not supposed to make in our rooms), and listened with tissues close at hand to our heartaches and worries. If you were to ask me to describe her, my immediate response would be, "She was a beautiful woman!" But when you took an honest look at Mrs. Jackson, you saw a woman with thinning hair streaked with gray, protruding front teeth, and wrinkles. Not a natural beauty. But we were attracted to and influenced by something I didn't have a name for then—the unnatural beauty of holiness.

Mrs. Jackson's life had not been easy. Her husband left for the mission field without her soon after they were married. Because of the dangers due to war, women were not permitted to go overseas at that time. She never saw her husband again. He was captured, tortured, and eventually died as a prisoner of war.

Mrs. Jackson chose not to allow her circumstances to make her bitter, but instead to allow God to use them to make her beautiful—and beautiful she was.

Mrs. Jackson had what God desired from the nation of Israel, what He desires from us—a deep love for Him alone. The path to holiness demands an undivided heart with one object of our love and commitment. The beauty of holiness can never exist apart from a deep and exclusive love with the source of all holiness—God alone!

Personal Reflection and Prayer

What are some idols worshiped in our culture?

There was a commercial years ago that asked, "How's your love life?" How does the correlation between our love of God and the beauty of holiness make this a valid question for us today?

Dear Loving Father,

Love has always been the basis of our relationship with You. No wonder You said it's the most important commandment. If we look at our call to holiness apart from love, we are left with the bondage of legalism. Free us from any idols so we may love You with a pure and passionate love. Amen.

Chapter Six

God's Alone

"Be absolutely His!" ~Oswald Chambers

Wholly is a homophone for holy—a word that sounds the same but has a different meaning and spelling. But it's also an important key to the beauty of holiness.

True holiness cannot be displayed in a life that isn't wholly God's. We are not only to worship God alone, but we are to be God's alone. Again, we see this in the history of the nation of Israel as God continually expressed His desire for them to be a holy nation. The problem was Israel kept forgetting this wasn't possible apart from being God's alone. Over and over again they became like the nations around them. Over and over again God would call them back to an exclusive relationship with Him. He was to be their God and they were to be His people—His alone!

Listen to God's words as He expressed the relationship between being wholly His and being holy. "I will be their God, and they will be my people. *Then* the nations will know that I the LORD make Israel holy" (Ezekiel 37:27–28 emphasis added). These words were spoken to a nation in exile because of their refusal to be God's alone. God was assuring them He would bring them back so that, once again, they would worship God alone and be God's alone.

Part of being God's alone was that God could do with them as He liked. God reminded the nation of Israel of this by using an example familiar to them. He was to be the potter and they were to be the clay. We hear His heart as He cries out to His people, "Can I not do with you, Israel, as this potter does?" (Jeremiah 18:6) He needed to be able to exercise the rights of the potter as they yielded to His plans for them. This could only happen if they were, like clay, pliable to His purpose, to His hands, as He formed them into what He desired them to be. Because Israel was God's alone, He had the exclusive rights of a potter.

Isaiah asked: "Does the clay say to the potter, 'What are you making?'" (Isaiah 45:9). God spoke this truth again through the prophet Jeremiah who declared, "LORD, I know that people's lives are not their own; it is not for them to direct their steps" (Jeremiah 10:23). Both show a clear picture of being wholly God's—of allowing Him to mold and direct as He sees best. Andrew Murray expresses the same thought. "Because He is the only God, He alone has a right to demand that we be wholly for Him."[14]

What was true for the nation of Israel is still true for us today. This idea is repeated in the New Testament when Paul asks, "But who are you…to talk back to God? Shall what is formed say to the one who formed it, 'Why did you make me like this?'" He goes on to ask, "Does not the potter have the right?" (Romans 9:20-21).

"Does not the potter have the right?" Paul gives us a clear answer to that question in the familiar words of 1 Corinthians 6:19. He reminds us we are God's temple. But those words are followed by this declaration: "You are not your own." That's a pretty strong statement, and one we often find hard to accept. We may agree with this theologically but resist this truth in the daily reality of our lives.

We want to know exactly what the Potter is doing. We want to direct our own steps. We want to be consulted and have veto power. We don't mind being His, but not wholly His. We don't mind co-operating, but we don't want to yield in absolute surrender. Andrew Murray reminds us "It is only the fully surrendered heart that can fully trust God for all He has promised."[15]

Oswald Chambers once challenged a friend with these words: "Be absolutely His!"[16] Imagine what our lives would be like if we truly were absolutely His. I looked up the word *absolutely* in the dictionary, and each definition adds so much more emphasis to that thought. Be unconditionally, wholly, positively, definitely, completely, unquestionably, and totally His. What a privilege to give ourselves in this way to a God whose love is limitless and whose ways are perfect.

The most forceful display of this surrender is found in the example of Christ. As He modeled life on Earth for us, He repeatedly declared His dependence on and obedience to the Father. Jesus says in John 14:31, "I love the Father and do *exactly* what my Father has commanded me" (emphasis added). The man Jesus never got in the way of the God Jesus. He was totally surrendered to God's will and God's plan. Jesus was wholly God and wholly God's.

There's no greater proof of this than Gethsemane. The anguished plea of Jesus to be spared the suffering our redemption required was immediately followed by, "Yet not as I will, but as You will" (Matthew 26:39). Those words may be the most important words ever uttered. Those words changed history and have the power to change lives. And those words from the lips of Jesus declared His absolute surrender to the Father.

The truth is God has every right to ask this of us. First, He's our creator and the sustainer of our every breath. Scripture reminds us "in him we live and move and have our being" (Acts 17:28). Our very existence is totally dependent on Him.

We also bear the image of our Creator. There's a New Testament story where Jesus was asked a question intended to trip him up. The question was a simple one, but with political and social ramifications. Did they need to pay taxes to Caesar? If you're familiar with the story, you know the wisdom of Jesus' answer. Taking a coin, he pointed out that it bore the image and mark of Caesar and therefore they should "give back to Caesar what is Caesar's, and to God what is God's" (Matthew 22:21). When relating this story, Ravi Zacharias asked simply, "Whose image is on you?" If Caesar can lay claim to what bears his image, how much more the Almighty God?

God is also the Supreme Sovereign over everything—including us. The name "King of kings and Lord of lords" is more than a nice title we give Him. It's an accurate expression of who He is. Scripture reminds us repeatedly that He has no equal—that no other being can even be compared to Him. David declares, "There is no one like you, LORD, and there is no God but you" (1 Chronicles 17:20). God Himself asks, "To whom will you compare me? Or who is my equal?" (Isaiah 40:25). He is greater than the sum total of our greatest thoughts about Him. He is not only beyond the scope of our understanding, but beyond the scope of our imagination. He is God. Greater than any definition or description. And He is the "blessed and only Ruler" (1 Timothy 6:15) and, as such, has every right to expect us to be wholly His.

My husband often remarks in moments of annoyance or frustration, "If I were the benevolent dictator of the world…" The truth of the matter is we already have a benevolent dictator. We can trust God's absolute rule because we can trust His absolute goodness and love.

These are many important and valid reasons for us to be God's alone, but one reason stands above all others and should cause us to bow in absolute surrender. He is our Redeemer.

I grew up in the era of hymns, and one I remember being sung often at the close of a service was "Fully Surrendered." The words of this hymn express the reason for His claim on us. "All on the altar laid, Surrender fully made, Thou hast my ransom paid, I yield to Thee."[17]

"Thou hast my ransom paid" is a line that takes away any claim I may have on myself. At great cost, and in a display of unfathomable love, Christ redeemed us. There can be no other appropriate response to that than, "I yield to Thee." Paul reminds us of this truth when he says, "You are not your own" and then quickly silences any argument we may have with the simple truth: "you were bought at a price" (1 Corinthians 6:19–20).

We are surrendering to One who paid the ultimate price for us. Another verse from the same hymn declares, "All, all belong to Thee, For Thou didst purchase me, Thine evermore to be, Jesus, my Lord."[18] I realize these words are outdated, but the truth they convey isn't. We have been purchased by God to be His alone for His purposes and His glory. And one of His purposes is that those around us see the beauty of His holiness displayed in our lives.

He has every right to us, and yet He doesn't insist on our surrender or demand it. He asks. We are given a choice. We are not forced to be wholly His. We can insist on having our own way, on making our own choices, on living based on our own desires, but these will never lead to holiness. We can work hard to be good and do good, but this alone is not holiness. Holiness cannot be experienced apart from being wholly God's. "We have as much of holiness as we have of God."[19]

In *C. S. Lewis and the Bright Shadow of Holiness,* Gerard Reed shares this: "Christian 'perfection' is in fact quite down-to-earth and doable. The singular and eminently attainable goal for which we should strive, C. S. Lewis taught, is holiness: the sincere soul-surrender that unites us with God and the developing virtuous character that results from that union."[20]

The good news is that to fully surrender to God has no risks. We are placing ourselves in the hands of a Potter who knows exactly what He's doing. We are yielding to One whose ways are perfect. Psalm 18:30 declares, "As for God, his way is perfect." Most of us wouldn't argue with that truth. But in verse 32 we're told God is also the One who makes our way perfect. I don't know about you, but I know I can't make my life perfect. I can't make choices that are always right and best. And I certainly can't mold myself into a usable vessel. He can!

I remember a young lady in one of our churches who absolutely would not surrender to God. She was convinced that if she did, He would send her to Africa and she did not want to go to Africa. She had such a skewed idea of God's willingness to make her life perfect. She believed that to surrender meant He would immediately insist on the very thing she dreaded the most and so decided to stick with her own choices. She was convinced her choices would be better and knew they would definitely not include Africa. I'm sure you can guess the rest of the story. Her choices ended up not being best. I doubt if God would have sent her to Africa, but even if He had, it would have been far better than where her own choices led her. All God wanted was for her to be His alone so He could make her way perfect.

No wonder Romans 12:1 makes it clear that to choose surrender makes sense—it's our "reasonable service" (KJV) or our "rational (logical, intelligent) act of worship" (The Amplified New Testament). Young's expresses it as "your intelligent service." In other words, in makes perfect sense to be wholly God's. Corrie Ten Boom says, "Surrender to the Lord is not a tremendous sacrifice, nor an agonizing performance; it is the most sensible thing you can do."[21] Surrender is the path to holiness. We can't be holy apart from being wholly His, and the choice is ours.

The hymn "Fully Surrendered" ends with these words: "Christ, all in all."[22] It can never be through our own efforts, but by allowing Christ to be all to us (God alone!) and all in us (God's alone). That's the key to the beauty of holiness.

Personal Reflection and Prayer

Being God's alone gives Him exclusive rights to you. How does the image of the potter show us this truth? How does the clay demonstrate surrender? (Reread Romans 9:20–21.)

Dear Sovereign God,

There is absolutely no risk in yielding to You—in being Yours alone. When we get a true glimpse of who You are—Your love, Your goodness, Your wisdom—we understand that being Yours completely is the wisest and most wonderful choice we can make. We are safe under Your love and care. Amen.

Chapter Seven

Devoted to Nearness

"God wills that we should push on into His presence
and live our whole life there." ~A.W. Tozer

The book of Jeremiah is considered by some to be depressing. Written by the prophet Jeremiah, also known as the weeping prophet, it is a warning to the nation of Israel of impending doom—not a message the Israelites wanted to hear. God makes it clear this is not because He's harsh or unjust, but that Israel alone is responsible for His wrath and judgment. "Your own conduct and actions have brought this on you" (Jeremiah 4:18).

But God's message of wrath and doom ends with a message of hope and restoration. God reminds His people of His heart for them in the familiar words of Jeremiah 29:11. "'For I know the plans I have for you,' declares the LORD, 'plans to prosper you and not to harm you, plans to give you hope and a future.'" God's judgment is tempered with His mercy.

In this case, His mercy includes the promise that Israel will come back to their own land. They will no longer be subject to a foreign king, but "Their leader will be one of their own; their ruler will arise from among them" (Jeremiah 30:21). That was good news! But God also makes clear the relationship He desires to have with this leader. "I will bring him near and he will come close to me" (verse 21).

God knew the nation of Israel well. He knew their pattern of rebellion, followed by repentance and well-intentioned promises. And He knew how quickly they failed to keep those promises. He knew their history of leaders that led His people away from a relationship with Him and enticed them with the worship of other gods. Israel was to stand apart as a holy nation. They were to display God's holiness to the nations around them—to show to others the purity and greatness of their God. God knew the only hope of this began with a leader who would draw near to Him.

Then God asks an important question—one as important to us today as it was back in Jeremiah's day. God asks, "who is he who will devote himself to be close to me?" (verse 21). Other translations suggest He is reminding them no one would dare draw near unless invited by God. Once again, He shows them their unique position as a nation privileged to have this relationship with a holy God—a nation that had been chosen for this very purpose.

"Who is he who will devote himself to be close to me?" In this question we hear the passion and desire of God's heart for His people. He wants to be in a relationship with them. He longs for them to be devoted to drawing near to Him. His purpose for Israel that they be a holy nation depended entirely on their commitment to a close and intimate relationship with Him—one that doesn't come from good intentions, but from a heart devoted to this pursuit.

Merriam-Webster Collegiate Dictionary defines *devote* as "to commit by a solemn act." But the Hebrew word has a far stronger meaning. It infers a giving over, even to the point of death. There is nothing half-hearted about the question God is asking, and He expects nothing half-hearted in their response. Drawing near to God must be their priority above everything else. Other things have to die or give way to this commitment of drawing near to God.

My niece Cherie decided to run a fifty-mile marathon. You read that right—a fifty-mile marathon. For months prior to the race Cherie spent hours running in preparation. If it rained, Cherie ran. If it was cold, Cherie ran. Day and night, Cherie ran. She was *devoted* to running this race, and her own comfort and desires had to give way to this pursuit.

When my husband and I watch the Olympics, we especially enjoy hearing the personal stories of the athletes—stories of what it cost them physically, financially, or mentally to pursue their dream. There are some who have had to leave family and friends to train under just the right coach. They are willing to sacrifice these things because they are devoted to their sport and their dream of winning the gold.

We were particularly struck by the story of a young ice-skater. He surprised everyone by his performance—even beating another American who was favored to win. It was no surprise when you heard the obstacles he had to overcome, the determination to focus on nothing but his skating for the years prior to the Olympics. Nothing else mattered and the results were a gold medal!

The next Olympic Games were a different matter. He had become involved in other interests. He still cared about skating, but his time was divided between skating and other pursuits. He had lost his passion and devotion to his sport, and it clearly showed in his performance.

God wanted Israel to have that passion and devotion to draw near to Him. He knew they couldn't be the holy nation He desired without this intimate relationship with Him. He longed for them to by holy—not just for their sake, but for the sake of His holy name. God makes His reason clear to the His people: "It is not for your sake, people of Israel, that I am going to do these things, but for the sake of my holy name...Then the nations will know that I am the LORD" (Ezekiel 36:22,23). God explains this will happen when "I am proved holy through you before their eyes" (vs. 23). The only way for this to happen was for them to draw near to Him.

The same is true for us. The beauty of holiness God desires to see displayed in our lives can only come from a close relationship with a holy God. It begins with yearning for an intimate relationship with God, and it is maintained with that same devotion and passion. As with Israel, this is not for our sake alone, but for the sake of our children, our co-workers, our neighbors who need to see the beauty of God's own holiness evident in our daily lives.

How do we draw near to God? This sounds nice in theory, but how do we live out the reality of this? What does this mean in our daily lives? We have to begin by answering God's question of "Who is he who will devote himself to be close to me?" with an upraised hand. It's me! I'm the one who desires this above all else and am willing to sacrifice other things for this pursuit.

It begins with desire but becomes a reality through devotion. In practical terms, it may mean less computer time and more time in the Word. It may mean less social media time and more time alone with God. It may mean less time in front of the television and more time on your knees. The things that had to give way in Cherie's life as she prepared for her fifty-mile marathon weren't bad things, they just had to take second place to her pursuit of her goal. Our use of time reflects our priorities. Never could there be a more worthwhile pursuit!

When Cherie was devoting herself to the goal of running a fifty-mile marathon, when the Olympians pursue their goal of achieving the gold medal, there is no guarantee of the outcome. (Cherie did successfully run all fifty miles.) However, when we choose to pursue a close relationship with the Almighty, we are assured of the outcome. James 4:8 gives us the surety if we devote ourselves to drawing near to God, He will respond by drawing near to us.

My son shared a wonderful illustration of this verse in a recent sermon. A few years ago, he took a team on a missions trip to Haiti. Among the group was Tim, a man who had spent many years in Haiti working in an orphanage. He became "father" to a group of precious little girls and was excited and nervous about seeing them again. Because they had not been told the truth about the circumstances of his leaving, he was uncertain of what their response would be. Here's my son's account of that moment.

"We pulled in and got out of the vans and a group of kids was out playing in the field next to the school. Several of Tim's girls were there. It was immediately apparent that they saw him. I looked over at Tim, expecting him to run to the girls, but he simply stood where he was. One of the girls threw her book bag down and began to run toward Tim, soon followed by others. He immediately responded and ran toward his *daughters*. And then it was all hugs, giggles, and tears. My entire team was in tears as we watched. I remember thinking that Tim had demonstrated more love by not moving. He let those girls choose. The minute they chose to draw near, Tim moved.

"That's the moment this verse took on new meaning for me. God loves us enough to give us the choice. When we make the slightest move toward drawing near, God makes up the distance and can't wait to wrap us in His arms. It's not a matter of Him not loving us enough to take the first step, it's a matter of Him loving us enough to let us take the first step, to let us make the choice of the intimacy of relationship that has always been His desire."

But there's more to that story. Tim had already taken a huge step. He had paid the price of an airline ticket, left his job and family, and made the trip to Haiti. The first move had been his, but then he waited for the girls to choose to respond to his presence.

The parallel is obvious. God has already taken a huge first step. His own Son left His home and paid an unbelievable price to come to us. But, like Tim, He gives us the choice to draw near.

This desire for a close relationship was initiated by God, but He will never force it on us. Like Tim, He immediately and lovingly responds when we make that first move to devote ourselves to nearness. God desires this because He loves us and longs for us to enjoy a close and intimate relationship with Him.

The beauty of holiness can only be seen in us as we spend time in the presence of the Holy One. Holiness is not something we achieve, but rather Someone we reveal, and that can't come from a casual relationship with God. It comes by running to Him—by throwing down our "book bags" and whatever else would slow us down and running right into His presence. It is not the pursuit of holiness that produces the beauty of holiness, but the pursuit of God.

A.W. Tozer says, "Ransomed men need no longer pause in fear to enter the Holy of Holies. God wills that we should push on into His Presence and live our whole life there."[23]

I think we see a beautiful illustration of this in the picture of the sparrow in Psalm 84:3. "Even the sparrow has found a home…a place near your altar, LORD Almighty, my King and my God." I'm sure other birds flew into the temple on occasion, but this one decided to build her nest there. She didn't want to just flit in and out, she wanted to live there. She *devoted* herself to making that her home.

God invites us to live continually in His presence. The sparrow's choice was evident by her nest. Where is your nest? Where do you live? Are you satisfied to just flit in and out of God's presence, or are you building your home there? Perhaps these are questions we all need to ask ourselves. Can we truthfully say, "I will give myself over completely, above all else, to being close to God—to building my nest in His presence?"

"Who is he who will devote Himself to draw close to me?" What an amazing question for the Almighty God to ask. It seems like the obvious answer should be, "Who wouldn't?" And yet, what was true for the nation of Israel is often true for us. We ignore this amazing invitation to draw near. It's important to remember the beauty of holiness is never attained through effort, but through gazing. It is as we draw near to God and look "full in His wonderful face," that we catch our breath in the wonder of His holiness and long for that unnatural beauty to be reflected in our own lives.

For years I've kept a quote by Robert Murray M'Cheyne in the front of my Bible. In these words we hear the longing of his heart to draw near to God.

"Oh, for the closest communion with God, till soul and body, head, face and heart—shine with Divine brilliancy! But oh! for a holy ignorance of our shining!"[24]

I don't know if there's a better description of the beauty of holiness and its source. It is in drawing near for the "closest communion" that we see and reflect this unnatural beauty—the beauty of holiness.

Personal Reflection and Prayer

Read Hebrews 10:19–22. What is the basis for our drawing near to God? Take some time to consider the immense price that was paid for this privilege. How does this truth impact the importance of drawing near to God?

Dear Heavenly Father,

Paul reminds us of the cost You paid for us to draw near to You—a price too costly for us to be content with just a casual relationship with You. And You invite us—encourage us—to draw near. Help us to take full advantage of this amazing privilege. Amen.

Chapter Eight

A Reflected Beauty

"[Holiness] is a thing utterly impossible unless we take time and allow the holiness of God to shine on us." ~Andrew Murray

It was Open House at my sons' elementary school. First, I went to my youngest son Steven's classroom where I met his teacher and, with proper parental pride, examined the papers laid out on his desk. Steven then took me to a bulletin board where, thumb-tacked to the board, were pictures drawn by each first grader of their mother. The freckled face of my six-year-old artist looked up at me expectantly as he asked, "Can you tell which one is you?" I looked back at the bulletin board and every picture looked pretty much the same—an oval face, two circles for eyes, a smaller circle for the nose, a curved line for the mouth, with some squiggly lines for hair.

Which one was me? I wore glasses at the time, which narrowed down the selection somewhat, so I hesitantly pointed to one with glasses. Steven's crestfallen face said it all. I had picked the wrong mother. He pointed to another masterpiece with a look that clearly indicated he was baffled that I could miss the obvious resemblance.

Next, I went to my son Dan's second grade classroom. I met the teacher, looked over an array of impressive papers on Danny's desk, and, once again, was led to a bulletin board. There, thumbtacked to the board, were some photographs of mothers who had recently been helpers in Danny's class. One of the photos was of me. There was no need for him to ask me to pick the right one. I recognized myself immediately. I didn't like it much more than Steven's rendition of my face, but there was no denying it was me.

What was the difference? The difference was that one was a child's interpretation, the other was a reflection. Steven drew his concept of me with the limited artistic skill of a first grader. Dan's teacher had taken a picture that was a reflected image of my face. The camera can only reveal what it sees.

God's desire has always been for His holiness to be displayed through His people. He made that clear repeatedly to Israel, and it is clearly His message to us today. We are not to *draw* our impression of God to other people; we are to reflect Him. Our drawings will always be a poor depiction of the Almighty, limited by the lack of the artistic ability of a finite being to reveal the infinite. But, just as the camera reflected an accurate picture of me, God can be clearly revealed as His reflection is seen in us.

Recently I sat overlooking a lake and was struck by the beauty of the sun's reflection on the water. It looked like a million sparkling diamonds. Then I began to think about that water. I've gone swimming in it, skipped stones on it (with limited success), and have seen it up close and personal. It's not beautiful water. In fact, it usually looks plain and brown. The difference today was the reflection of the sun that transformed the ordinary water of the lake into a thing of beauty.

The illustration is obvious. We have no holiness of our own. We can't achieve it by our own efforts no matter how earnest and sincere. We simply can't be holy! Over and over as God was giving the Law to the nation of Israel, he reminded them the Law would never make them holy. He alone was holy, and He alone could make them holy. The beauty of holiness truly is a beauty that isn't natural to us. It's one that can only be seen as God's own holy image is reflected through us.

I think the closest parallel we can find is one God gives us in nature. The moon has no light of its own. There's nothing in the moon capable of being a source of light. However, when it is lined up where it can "see" the sun, it is able to reflect the light of the sun.

Second Corinthians 3:18 NLT is a favorite verse of mine. "So all of us who have had that veil removed can see and reflect the glory of the Lord." Holiness is not accomplished by effort, but by gazing. We are as helpless to produce our own holiness as the moon is to produce its own light. There's nothing else that can transform us simply in response to our gaze. This is a work of God alone with no earthly equal or rival. It is the secret of the unveiled face. As we gaze, we are transformed into a beautiful reflection of His holiness!

The New Unger's Bible Dictionary states "God's glory is the correlative of his holiness…is that in which his holiness comes to expression."[25] In this verse, Paul urges us to reflect the Lord's glory—His holiness. He reminds us twice in these few words that it's not a glory that originates in us but is a glory that comes exclusively from the Lord.

Just as the camera reflected my image, just as the lake reflected the light of the sun, just as the moon reflects the light of the sun, we are to reflect God in all His glory. He is asking for us to display, through our lives, an accurate reflection of who He is so others will be drawn to Him. The beauty of holiness is His and is to be evident for His purposes and His glory. What a privilege! What a responsibility!

Paul draws this illustration from the life of Moses. Soon after Moses had found the Israelites worshipping the golden calf, God instructed him he was to lead the people out from there. God then informed Moses He was not going with them but would send an angel as their guide. Moses already realized leading these people wasn't going to be an easy job. He also knew it was one he didn't want to attempt without the assurance of God's presence. And so, Moses simply responds that if God isn't going, neither is he. Because of His love for Moses, God relents and agrees to go with them.

God's assurance of His presence seemed to give Moses the courage to ask for even more and so he requests, "Now show me your glory" (Exodus 33:18). And God did. In an amazing scene, God hides Moses in a rock and from that vantage point, Moses gets a glimpse of the glory and wonder of God.

But the wonderful thing is God didn't just answer that request with one incident. Later, when Moses returned from his second trip up Mount Sinai, his face displayed such a radiant reflection of the glory of God it frightened the Israelites, and Moses veiled his face until the glory faded.

Now Paul is assuring us we no longer need to cover our faces. We have the amazing privilege of reflecting that same glory—that same display of God's holiness—to those around us with unveiled faces.

The simple and obvious truth is that, like a camera, we can't reflect what we don't see. A familiar verse urges us to run the race of life while "fixing our eyes on Jesus" (Hebrews 12:2). The Amplified Bible, Classic Edition expresses it this way: "Looking away (from all that will distract) to Jesus."

These are more than just a few extra words added to the text. These words share a deeper meaning taken from the original Greek word that means "to look away from one thing so as to see another; to concentrate the gaze upon."[26] We can't reflect the beauty of God's holiness by an occasional glance. It means looking away from other things that would distract and fixing our eyes—concentrating our gaze—on Jesus.

Our lives are full of distractions. We're surrounded by things that would keep our eyes from being continually focused on the Lord. Often, we settle for a glance in His direction on Sunday during worship or quickly look His way when there's time during the week. Even when our intentions are good, life interferes, and we find ourselves occupied with the demands and busyness of daily living. We have jobs and families and, in the midst of all of that, how do we make fixing our eyes on Jesus real and practical?

We find an answer in the reminder that this is, above all else, a love relationship. Jesus made this clear when He declared the greatest commandment was to simply love the Lord with all our heart, soul, and mind. It brings us right back to the truth that holiness is not a result of our behavior but stems from an intimate relationship with a holy God. It comes from loving, rather than doing.

It's impossible to separate the beauty of holiness from a deep and intimate love relationship with God. It's possible to be pious and religious without love. It's possible to obey the "rules" of our church, to conform to the Christian standards for the day, to fit in with the social norm of being a Christian all without love. But it's not possible to display the true beauty of holiness apart from a vibrant love relationship with a holy God.

Amy Carmichael reminds us "even the least of us can be a lover." God has made this relationship available to all of us—even the least of us. It's the thread that binds all of Scripture together. It begins in the Garden of Eden and culminates in the glories of heaven. I can think of no good reason why God should love us, but I can think of endless reasons why our hearts should overflow with love for Him.

It's love that draws our eyes to Him. It's love that finds no greater joy than drawing near to God and fixing our eyes on Him as we spend time in His presence. And it's love that allows us to reflect His glory—His holiness—to those around us.

Amy Carmichael tells of taking a group of Indian children to watch a goldsmith at work. As they watched him go through the various stages of refining the gold, she finally asked him when he knows it's pure. His response was, "When I can see my face in it."[27]

God has that same desire for us. He longs to see His face reflected in us. An old chorus expresses it so well. "Let the beauty of Jesus be seen in me, All His wonderful passion and purity. O, Thou Spirit Divine, all my nature refine, 'til the beauty of Jesus be seen in me."[28]

We can't produce the beauty of holiness, even with our most sincere desire and most determined effort. But we can, with unveiled faces, reflect a beauty that originates with God—the beauty of His holiness.

Personal Reflection and Prayer

How does the illustration of the moon help us to understand the beauty of holiness? During a lunar eclipse, Earth comes between the sun and the moon, blocking the sunlight falling on the moon. What are some things in your life that eclipse the Son and hinder the beauty of God's pure holiness from being reflected in your life?

Dear Father,

We have no natural beauty of holiness. No matter how hard we try, we can't produce it. And we can't reflect what we cannot see. Help us to remove anything that would obstruct our view of You so others may see the beauty of Your reflected holiness in our lives. Amen.

Chapter Nine

Unveiled Faces

"If we do not want those veils, He will clear
them away." ~Amy Carmichael

One of the most anticipated moments in many weddings
comes after the bridesmaids and flower girl have made their
way down the aisle to the front of the church. The music suddenly
changes, people immediately stand to their feet and turn to watch
as the bride enters and begins her walk down the aisle. She has
spent months, and often a great deal of money, for this moment.
As her groom waits in the front of the church, he sees the one he
loves coming toward him with a veil covering her face. He can
see her, but not clearly. Then comes a moment in the wedding
ceremony when the veil is finally lifted, and he looks full into the
face of the women he has chosen to be his wife.

Imagine the husband's frustration if his wife decided never to
remove her veil. Imagine his disappointment in not ever getting
a clear image of his wife—of not seeing her face without the
limitations and distortions of a veil? His understandable desire as

a husband is to see his wife with an unveiled face.

In 2 Corinthians 3:18, Paul reminds us we are to reflect the Lord's glory with unveiled faces—with nothing to hinder or blur His image. We're to remove anything that would keep us from accurately reflecting the glory of God.

We're all born with a veil covering our face. It's a veil that has been passed down since the days of Adam and Eve when sin entered the world. And it's a veil that can't be removed by our best intentions and most earnest efforts. This veil of sin doesn't just distort the image of God, it hinders us from seeing Him at all. We're reminded of the seriousness of this in Isaiah 59:2, "your sins have hidden his face from you."

But what we can't do, God has done for us. In His great love, He has provided a way for this veil to be forever removed through the death and resurrection of His own Son. Just like that moment in a wedding, there's a moment when we say yes to God's offer of forgiveness and He lovingly lifts the veil of sin from us. Finally, we're able to "look full in His wonderful face."[29]

But even after this dark veil has been removed, we often put on other veils that distort the image of God. One I've seen often worn by women I've counseled is the veil of shame or guilt. They know they're a child of God. They know they've been forgiven. But they still live with the shame of past sins—of wrong choices, of mistakes, and sinful behavior. The problem with the veil of shame is it keeps us from wanting to look full into God's face.

Several years ago, we had a cute little dog named Andy. Andy was a good dog, most of the time. Like many dogs, he was destitute when we went away and ecstatic when we returned—except when he had been bad. When he didn't come bounding to meet us, we knew there was a problem. When we called his name, he would slink toward us, head down. Even if we took his little head and lifted it up, he would avert his eyes. He was covered in shame and we knew we'd better go look around to see what he had done.

The veil of shame and guilt causes that same reaction in us, and we can't reflect God if we're not looking at Him. Scripture makes it clear this is a veil we no longer need to wear. God offers full forgiveness for sin—including the shame and the guilt associated with it. I love the assurance of Psalm 34:5. "Those who look to him are radiant; their faces are never covered with shame." Psalm 32:5 assures us God not only forgives our sins but forgives "the guilt of my sin."

These words were written by a sinner. David knew from his own life and experience the shame and guilt of sin. But he also knew of God's complete forgiveness that allowed him to remove the veil of shame and guilt and look freely into the face of God.

Another veil frequently worn is that of worry. Life offers us many valid reasons for worry, but these are negated by the promises and assurance of a loving Heavenly Father. This veil distorts the image of God and reveals Him as a God who can't be trusted; a God who either doesn't care enough or isn't powerful enough to take care of our concerns.

The verses that reassure us of God's willingness and ability to care for our every need are too numerous to mention, but even one is enough. God assures us in Philippians 4:19 He will supply all our needs based on His own supply and riches in Christ Jesus. That truth alone is enough to remove the veil of worry and allow an all-sufficient God to be clearly seen.

We are reminded in that same chapter of Philippians to "be anxious for nothing" (Philippians 4:6 NKJV). That's a tall order and one we often find hard to put into practice. But notice the context of these words. They're preceded by the assurance "the Lord is near" and followed by how we are to respond. We are to bring everything—all our worries, all our fears, all our anxieties— to God with thanksgiving. It is that act that removes the veil of worry. It is that choice that allow others to see a God who can be trusted in all circumstances.

Amy Carmichael encourages us to remove the veil of worry with these words: "There are reasons and reasons for hope and happiness, and never one for fear."[30] Amy's missionary life included many times when the veil of worry would have seemed justified, but she refused to wear it and offers us through her life and writing a glimpse of a faithful and trustworthy God.

One of my favorite chapters to write in my book *The Sweet Side of Suffering* was "The Sweetness of His Care." My husband and I were going through a frightening time at the writing of that chapter and the veil of worry seemed to be glued to my face. As I wrote example after example of God's provision and faithfulness in the past, I felt the veil of worry lift as I looked into the face of the One who remains faithful.

There's also the veil of an unforgiving spirit or bitterness. Over the years I have seen many women who cling to this veil. They feel the hurt or the pain they've experienced justifies it and are reluctant to take it off.

I remember counseling a woman who had experienced some deep hurts from the very person who should have protected her— her mother. As she shared her childhood with me, she ended with these emphatic words: "Don't ever expect me to forgive her!" She had earned that veil and was determined to wear it for all to see. The problem was it kept her from accurately seeing the face of a loving and caring heavenly Father, and hindered others from seeing the healing power of God's grace reflected in her life.

How drastically this veil distorts the face of God. It reveals a God who is indifferent to human suffering. It masks the grace that is part of His beauty.

I don't make light of human suffering—of the very real pain that can come because of someone else's actions. But God has assured us we can live free of that veil. Those who hurt us must someday answer to Him. Those who have been harmed have the assurance of His personal and loving care. I love the verse that says, "In all their distress He too was distressed" (Isaiah 63:9). God is not indifferent to our pain. He shares in our human heartaches, but He longs for us to display a God who can bring freedom and healing. That image of God can't be seen through the veil of bitterness.

In my years of counseling women, another veil I've frequently seen is one of self-pity. Life hasn't been fair, people haven't treated them right, their circumstances aren't what they deserve, etc. The problem with this veil is it reveals a God who hasn't chosen what is best. A child of God should never say or feel, "Poor me!" The implications of that are God has made a mistake in your life; it reveals the image of an uncaring or unwise God. He is neither! It is only when the veil of self-pity is removed that God can be reflected as the loving and wise God He truly is.

Another veil that can cover our faces is that of lukewarmness. It can fall over our face so gradually we often don't realize it's there. We have a clear picture of God's response to that veil in Rev. 3:15, 16. God would prefer us be hot or cold rather than lukewarm and declares to the Church in Laodicea that "because you are lukewarm—neither hot nor cold—I am about to spit you out of my mouth." Lukewarmness leaves a bad taste in the mouth of the Almighty.

Seen through that veil, we display a God who is not worthy of our passionate love and devotion. God is seen as a nice extra in our life rather than life itself; a nice convenience rather than a consuming passion. A song by Larnelle Harris puts this all into perspective.

"He paid much too high a price for me;
Your tears, Your blood, the pain,
To have my soul just stirred at times and never really changed.

He deserves a fiery love that won't ignore His sacrifice because He paid much too high a price."[31]

He paid much too high a price for us to wear the veil of lukewarmness. He truly does deserve a fiery love that reveals to those around us a God worthy of our complete love and devotion.

In *The Wizard of Oz*, Dorothy and her friends are on a journey to find the great wizard they believe is the answer to each of their needs. When they arrive, they find him hidden behind a curtain. However, when the curtain falls, they discover, to their dismay, he is less—so much less—than they had imagined. The curtain was hiding the truth.

If we were able to pull back the curtain right now to reveal God in all His glory and fullness, He would be more—so much more—than we ever imagined. The veil of lukewarmness is like that curtain. It hinders those around us from seeing God as He is. He looks less holy, less powerful, less loving, less majestic and glorious—less than God. No wonder God responds the way He does to lukewarmness as it distorts the reality of His amazing greatness and glory.

The veil of self-righteousness is also one we often don't realize we're wearing. It's a veil that seems suited to a Christian, but greatly distorts the image of God's own true beauty and holiness. It's a veil that draws attention to us, a veil that seeks to impress others with our own goodness. While it may seem like a beautiful covering to us, God describes it as a veil made of filthy rags. The actual scriptural meaning of that term is very graphic but shows clearly how despicable this is to God. We may think we look good, but He doesn't. Our self-righteousness is a cheap imitation of the true righteousness of God.

We were getting ready to leave for Columbia, South America, to speak at a conference for missionaries. As we prepared to go, I had an uncomfortable sense things weren't completely right between God and me. I earnestly prayed for God to search my heart and reveal any area of sin that would hinder me from being used by Him at this conference. Finally, I sensed God saying, "Esther, it's not sin, it's your self-righteousness."

I wish I could have argued with Him, but I knew He was seeing in me a poor imitation of His own righteousness. It was a veil I had become very comfortable wearing, but one I earnestly wanted removed.

Words I had sung many times now became my prayer. "O to be saved from myself, dear Lord, O to be lost in Thee, O that it might be no more I, but Christ, that lives in me."[32] If ever there was a plea for the veil of self-righteousness to be removed it is found in these words. And if ever anyone needed that veil removed it was me.

God is faithful to show us the veils we're wearing. These veils are many and varied. Some, like the veil of disobedience, are dark and almost hide His face; others are hardly noticeable, but all distort His image. Some of these veils have been worn so long we hardly notice them. But we can trust the Lord to reveal them to us and help us remove them. The words of Amy Carmichael are an encouragement: "If the will be set towards beholding, looking, reflecting, then our Lord will see to the veils."[33]

God has called us to reflect Him, and He desires we do so with unveiled faces so others may see in us a clear reflection of the beauty of His holiness.

Personal Reflection and Prayer

Sometimes we become so accustomed to certain veils we forget we're wearing them. What veils do you wear? How are they distorting God's image to those around you? Take time to prayerfully ask God to reveal and remove any veils so He may be clearly and accurately reflected.

Dear Holy God,

So often our lives don't reveal the true wonder of who You are to those around us. We wear veils that distort Your image and hinder You from being seen in all Your beauty. We are surrounded by people who desperately need to see You—who need to know You as You truly are. Remove our veils so Your true beauty can be seen reflected in us. Amen.

Chapter Ten

The Ultimate Beauty Treatment

"To stand before the Holy One of eternity
is to change." ~Richard Foster

It's fun to watch a makeover on television. Usually someone is chosen with hair that's too long, little or no makeup, and wearing clothes that reflect a lack of style. Then the beauty treatment begins, and for a few hours the recipient is the center of attention by hairdressers, make-up artists, and experts on style and fashion. Then the big reveal as the audience gasps at the change and family members hardly recognize their loved one.

It's typical for a beauty treatment to focus on the one being treated. When you go in for a beauty treatment, whether it's hair color, skin tone, or a manicure, it's all about you—about what looks best on you and what you prefer. However, the beauty treatment for the beauty of holiness is different in that it's only effective when our focus is not on ourselves, but on a holy God.

Genuine worship is the ultimate act of taking our attention from ourselves to the One whom we worship. Sadly, there is much debate and division in the Church today about worship. The very thing that should unite us, now often divides us. The very thing that should be about God has become about us. We once attended a church where the young people were silent and looked bored when hymns were sung, and the older people looked annoyed and refused to sing when the worship choruses were sung. Their style of worship had become more important than worship itself.

A few years ago, my husband and I moved to a new area and began the process of visiting local churches to find a church home. We visited everything from stained glass to strobe lights. It was quite an eye-opener to see the marketing that went on under the name of worship to attract people.

The stained-glass church was beautiful. The choir was amazing, the words read and preached were true, but there was a coldness and dryness that all the beautiful music and right words couldn't disguise.

The words "cold and dry" certainly didn't apply to the strobe light church. The appeal to younger people was evident as we looked at the hundreds of people gathered around us. However, we realized quickly very few of them were engaged in worship. Some were sipping coffee and chatting with their neighbors, others were busy on their phones. A man in front of us paid a bill online, and a young girl was working on her homework—all while "worship" was taking place.

What we wanted to find was a place where God was the focus. Since worship is supposed to be about Him, we wanted to find a church where He truly was the object of worship. I want to add that the problem with those other churches wasn't the more traditional setting of pews and stained glass, or the more contemporary setting of drums and lights. The problem was they forgot the One who was worthy of their total attention and worship. They forgot God!

We did finally find a church "by accident" one Sunday morning, but certainly by God's plan and direction. It wasn't the style of worship that attracted us; it was the experience of worship that drew us. That morning we heard it said several times, "Remember, this isn't about us. It's about directing our love and focus on God." God was continually held up and exalted. We had found a group of people who were worshipping, and we wanted to be a part of it.

I think it's significant that after God had established His place as Israel's only God, the next commandment sets the guidelines for worship. God makes it clear He expects worship to be an integral part of their lives as His children. They were to worship God alone. He knew His people would be surrounded by other nations that worshipped gods of their own making, and His place as the only true God dictated He alone was worthy of worship.

I don't believe the enemy cares if we engage in something we call worship (whether in the setting of stained glass or strobe lights) as long as our hearts aren't engaged in true worship. He doesn't mind how many choruses we sing, how high our hands are raised, how sincere we look to others, as long as we aren't bowed in worship before a holy God.

God is the reason for our worship. He is the object of our worship. And to come into His presence invokes the natural response of worship.

One misconception about worship is that it takes place in a church surrounded by other Christians. Often it does. But the best corporate worship is when a group of worshippers—those for whom this is part of their daily experience with God—join their voices together to acknowledge the greatness and worthiness of our God. Corporate worship should never be our only worship experience. Worship needs to be a vital part of the personal time we spend with God.

We attended a church that struggled with worship. They tried almost every worship style possible to no avail. They tried the traditional hymnbooks with organ and piano, the more contemporary words on a screen, for a while they had an orchestra, then a worship team. We were never sure what we would find from one week to the next. The problem wasn't the style; the problem was the participants. No matter how hard they tried, they weren't going to produce a sense of worship without worshippers.

Worship is one of the shortest routes into the presence of God. It's the best way to turn our eyes Godward and focus on Him. David encouraged us to "worship the LORD in the beauty of holiness" (Psalm 29:2 NKJV). If your heart's desire is to be holy, then spend time with its source in the presence of a holy, holy, holy God. Worship brings us into a holy atmosphere where we breathe out our love and worship and breathe in His holiness.

Make worship personal. The real test of your relationship to God is what takes place when it's just you and God. Years ago, a close friend of mine shared that her parents were getting a divorce. I was stunned. Her dad was a pastor and they seemed happily married. Then she shared this story with me. Sunday after Sunday her parents would go to the back of the church to greet the parishioners. Her mother would put her arm through her dad's. They would laugh and talk as they greeted members of their church family. And then they would go home, and not speak another word to one another.

If I were to ask which of those two scenes was the real indicator of their love, you would quickly respond it was what took place at home. And so it is with us. It's what takes place in our personal and private times with God that truly reflects our relationship with Him. Andrew Murray reminds us, "God must be first. To this end there must be secret prayer, where God and you alone can meet."[34] Public worship is a wonderful privilege, but it should be an overflow from the personal worship we've been experiencing all week.

I love to get cards from my husband. He claims to have "the gift of cards" and really does often find the perfect card for an occasion. He searches until he finds just the right card that expresses his heart. I have a box where I've saved many of the cards he's given me over the years, but my favorite part of those cards is the personal notes he writes at the end. The words may not be as poetic, but I love them because they are his own words used to express his heart. We're blessed with a history of hymns and wonderful worship choruses by gifted song writers, but don't forget to find time to express your own heart, in your own words, as you worship. My guess is while your own words may not be as poetic as some worship choruses, they bring great joy to the heart of God.

If you don't know where to begin, borrow from David; share in the overflow of his heart in the psalms and make his words your own. You can also use old worship hymns, new worship choruses, the names of God, or the attributes of God as a place to begin your personal worship. Use these to express your own heart and then add a personal note. There are many ways to worship, but one God to worship. Make worship a personal priority.

We go to a beauty treatment with the focus on ourselves and the hope we'll come away improved. We enter true worship with the focus rightfully on God and come away changed. It's the ultimate beauty treatment.

I referenced 2 Corinthians 3:18 in a previous chapter. It's a wonderful reminder of the privilege we have of reflecting God's holiness to others. But there's more that happens as we gaze at God with unveiled faces. The rest of the verse assures us our focus on God results in a change in us. As we gaze at Him in worship, we are "transformed into his image with ever-increasing glory." There is nothing else able to transform us simply in response to our gaze. This is a work of God alone with no earthly equal or rival. It is the secret of the unveiled face. As we gaze, we are transformed.

I've shared in other chapters about the revival that took place at Asbury College. The presence of God made us immediately aware of our own sins and failures, so confessions and cleansing were a big part of what took place. But there was also a continual spirit of intense worship. We were in God's presence and worship was a natural response. The confession cleansed us; the worship changed us.

The hymn-writer said when Christ comes, we will bow "in humble adoration, and there proclaim, 'My God how great Thou art!'"[35] Christ had come to Asbury and that's exactly what we did. We bowed in humble adoration and it was a worship experience I will never forget. We encountered a holy God and we were changed by that encounter.

Years ago, I was planning a prayer retreat for the women in our church. I called a friend who had led similar retreats to ask for some suggestions. During our conversation, he said four simple words that not only had great impact on our retreat but transformed my own prayer life as well. He said, "Always begin with worship."

Andrew Murray shares this same thought. "The first thing must be to bow in lowly reverence before God in His glory—the Father whose name is to be hallowed—and so offer Him your adoration and worship."[36] There are so many things that can change in our lives if we make worship a priority.

God has chosen us for a make-over and it takes place as we turn with unveiled faces to Him in worship. He promises that as we do, we will be "transformed into His likeness with ever-increasing glory, which comes from the Lord, who is the Spirit" (2 Corinthians 3:18). There simply is no greater beauty treatment than that!

Personal Reflection and Prayer

How would you define worship? What part does worship play in your personal time with God? How does worship impact the beauty of holiness in our lives? (Remember: It's not the *how* of worship that should be our focus, but the *who* of worship.)

Dear Holy God,

Worship brings us into Your presence, and a sense of Your presence evokes an outpouring of worship. And how like You that we come to give You worship, You give so much in return. May we learn those important four words and "always begin with worship." You alone are worthy! Amen.

Chapter Eleven

A Clean Temple

"He has bought us for the high price of the blood of Christ, and it's only fitting that we become structures worthy of the price." ~David Jeremiah

A door in the ladies' room of the church I attended as a little girl led to a place that was both scary and fascinating. Through that door was the church basement. One small overhead bulb did little to light up the space, but it did reveal the dust and cobwebs that made it a rather spooky room to a little girl. However, hidden away in the recesses of that basement was something that made it worth facing my fears—a large detailed replica of Solomon's temple. I was allowed to look, but not to touch. Even on this much smaller scale, it was impressive, and I loved to look at all the miniature details of this amazing structure.

Solomon built a magnificent temple. I think it's hard for our twenty-first century minds to grasp the opulence of the structure constructed as a dwelling place for Israel's God. We would quickly run out of adjectives in an attempt to accurately convey its splendor. It was a lavish display of magnificent handiwork of the finest material designed by master craftsmen. This was Yahweh's place—designed by Him for His glory.

Second Chronicles 7:1,2 relates a truly awesome moment for the nation of Israel. As Solomon dedicated this beautiful structure to God, God responded by filling the temple with His glory and presence. In fact, it says even the priests couldn't enter because the glory of God's presence was so overwhelming. There was room for nothing but God.

However, the history of this beautiful edifice is a sad one. This sense of God's presence and glory came to a heartbreaking end when Ezekiel shared that he watched as "the glory of the LORD departed from over the threshold of the temple" (Ezekiel 10:18).

There were times when the temple was used for the worship of other gods; times when the temple was neglected, and the altars grew cold. There were times when enemies came in and emptied the temple of its wealth and beauty. This magnificent place first became misused and then neglected. The grandeur was gone, and the glory of God had departed.

While those events took place many years ago, the temple still stands as an example and reminder of what can happen to a place set aside for God's presence. Paul reminds us that now we are that dwelling place. We are God's temple, the place where He longs to live and reveal His glory. And there are lessons we can learn from Solomon's temple—lessons that have great significance for us today.

If you're familiar with the Old Testament account of Israel's kings, you know they jockeyed back and forth from one king who did right in the sight of God to another who did evil in the sight of God. From time to time, one of the kings who followed God would decide to clean up and restore the temple. Hezekiah was one of those kings.

Scripture tells us it was in the first month of the first year of his reign that he opened the doors of the temple of the Lord and repaired them. He had watched his father Ahaz remove the furnishings of the temple and shut the doors, instead placing altars "at every street corner in Jerusalem" (2 Chronicles 28:24). Perhaps Hezekiah made a personal "campaign promise" to himself that if he ever became king, his first act would be to open the doors of God's temple and return it to its intended glory. And so he did.

Hezekiah instructed the Levites to remove all defilement from the sanctuary. They were to take out everything that didn't belong in God's holy dwelling place. Scripture tells us, "They brought out to the courtyard of the LORD's temple everything unclean that they found in the temple of the LORD" (2 Chronicles 29:16).

The next thing they did was to return all the furnishings and articles to their rightful place in the temple. They reported to the king they had "prepared and consecrated all the articles that King Ahaz removed in his unfaithfulness while he was king. They are now in front of the LORD's altar" (2 Chronicles 29:19). Everything was back where it belonged.

I think it's important to point out again that while this cleansing was very important, it wasn't cleaning up and having things in their place that made the temple holy. It was the presence of God. The temple was restored so that the holy, holy, holy God of Israel could take His rightful place among them.

What about us? What about the reality that we are now God's temple? What clutter do we have that needs to come out—what furnishings need to be put back in their rightful place? Do we need to repair the doors and walls to make it fit for the King of kings to fill it once again with His glory?

These are not abstract questions but present some very practical challenges. Those kings who repaired Solomon's temple didn't do so just to add one more spot for tourists to visit. They weren't looking to improve their ratings among the people. They were committed to getting rid of everything that hindered the presence of a holy God and bringing back everything that contributed to His worship.

Sanctification is a scriptural term that represents that cleansing process in the lives of God's temples today. It signifies a setting apart for a specific use. The Old Testament tabernacle had been built and sanctified as the dwelling place of God. It was to be a place set apart as the place to experience God's presence and respond to Him in worship and prayer.

Sanctification is God's will for His children. But sanctification does not produce the beauty of holiness; it cleanses us so God's holiness can be on display, unhindered and unencumbered. It removes debris and things that don't belong and brings back things that are conducive to the worship of the Almighty. It is a means to an end, and the end is God's presence revealed in and through us. The end is the beauty of God's own holiness.

Sanctification is different from introspection. Introspection is like trying to clean a room in the dark. Introspection fails because we aren't capable of knowing our own hearts (Jeremiah 17:9). It is instead, allowing the light of the Spirit to shine in our hearts to reveal the things that must be removed. Amy Carmichael expresses it this way: "The Search-light of the Spirit discovers us to ourselves, and such a discovery leaves us appalled."[37]

Sanctification is not about being better, it's about being cleansed. It's not about self-improvement, it's about self-denial. It's that process of being refined as gold so the goldsmith can see His face reflected in us.

For a number of years, I lived in a city with a well-deserved reputation for cloudy days. The "bright side" to cloudy days is that dirt doesn't show. My house, especially my windows, seemed much cleaner than they really were when there was no sun. But on the occasional sunny day, the truth was revealed. What appeared to be clean was in reality covered with fingerprints, smudges, and dust. It took the sunlight to reveal the truth.

Sometimes we prefer cloudy days rather than the sunny ones that reveal the true state of our temples. But Amy Carmichael reminds us "the light is not turned upon us to rob us of our hope."[38] The light of God's presence is what brought students and faculty to their knees in confession at Asbury. The light is what can show us the true state of our temple. And it's the light that brings us to the cleansing we need so we can display the unnatural beauty of God's own holiness.

Daniel shares his response to catching a glimpse of the "light" of God's glory in Daniel 10:8 KJV: "there remained no strength in me: for my comeliness was turned in me into corruption."

What a powerful description of what happens to a person in the manifest presence of God. All our "comeliness" (all we held to be good and appealing) evaporates instantly in the light of absolute holiness and we are left with the truth about our corrupt selves. It is in God's realized presence that all illusions are shattered. We see ourselves as we truly are and cry: "Woe *is* me!" (Isaiah 6:5 KJV).

Jeremiah reminds us our hearts are "deceitful above all things… Who can understand it?" (Jeremiah 17:9). In other words, we often don't know what junk there is in our hearts—things that have accumulated over the years of which we are often unaware. But the good news is found in the words of Jeremiah 17:10. "I the LORD search the heart." After reminding us of the deceitfulness of our own hearts, Jeremiah shares God's assurance that He will search our hearts for us. Even more wonderful is the assurance that if we are honest in admitting to the junk we find in our hearts, God Himself will "purify us from all unrighteousness" (1 John 1:9).

What is our part in this? We simply need to give God complete access to our "temple." It's part of acknowledging that we are completely His. We give Him the right to every part—even hidden parts we may not be aware of. Remember, our hearts are deceitful.

A wonderful example of temple cleansing is the revival at Asbury College that I mentioned in an earlier chapter. It began on an ordinary day during an ordinary chapel service. No one sitting in the auditorium that morning could have anticipated the chapel service wouldn't end until about twelve days later. Classes were cancelled, other activities stopped, because what was happening in Hughes Auditorium was more important than anything else— even eating.

What was happening in Hughes Auditorium? Simply put, God came to Asbury and few would ever be the same.

All these years later it is still hard to find words to adequately express the experience of entering God's manifest presence. While the experience defies words, the impact was very evident in the line of students, faculty, and visitors, waiting to confess and repent of the clutter and debris in their temples. The conviction and cleansing were all worth it just to be in God's presence. I didn't want to leave…and judging from the almost empty cafeteria, and empty classrooms, neither did anyone else.

That response was not because there was someone pleading and extolling them. That response was not because of many verses of an invitation hymn that was being sung. That response was the same as that of Isaiah's when confronted with the holiness of God. It was a response of, "Woe is me!" Things they had been willing to live with now became abhorrent to them and they pled for cleansing. Sins were confessed, relationships restored as temples were being cleansed.

Job was a righteous man. He lived a life committed to obedience to God and His law. To those around him, his life showed evidence of God's blessing. But things quickly changed as Job met with overwhelming loss and suffering. During these dark days, Job repeatedly declared if he could only meet with God he would argue his case, he would defend himself, he would ask God why.

But when Job did encounter God, he forgot all about pleading His case or questioning God. What Job did was repent. The manifest presence of God revealed things in Job's life that caused him to fall on his knees in sorrow and repentance. God's presence is so utterly holy it brings to light anything in our lives that is not holy.

Harold Spann notes, "Repentance is a complete house cleaning. There can be no compromise with sin. God will not put the beauty of His holiness on the bargain counter of man's carnal marketplace at a reduced price! Anything known to be an impediment to our character in Christ must be removed."[39]

We have an extra room upstairs in our house we use as a bedroom when our grandchildren arrive. In between their visits it becomes a storage room by default—a convenient place to put things that don't have a permanent resting place. Cleaning out the stuff that accumulates over time isn't always easy, but I gladly do it to make room for those amazing little people called grandchildren. When they arrive, the room is once again filled with stuff, but it's their stuff—things that are part of their presence in my home.

During the Asbury Revival, one student urged others to: "Shovel out the trash"—to "rid themselves of the old trash and garbage"[40] to make room for Jesus.

It's possible to take the words of this chapter and nod in abstract agreement. There is nothing abstract about this. God's desire to cleanse His temple is a most practical and real experience. It's hard. It's sometimes painful. It's often tedious. But it's always worth it.

I remember experiencing this in my own life while caring for my mother-in-law who was in her nineties and suffering from Alzheimer's. I didn't always care for her with the patience and kindness I should have. That was a real struggle for me as I've continually pled with the Lord to help me.

I wanted to be zapped with all the wonderful qualities of the fruit of the Spirit and was frustrated when that didn't happen. But what God did instead was to first shine His light in my heart to show me attitudes that were displeasing to Him. I didn't like what I saw, but I'm thankful for the love that prompted God to search the temple of my heart and reveal the junk that needed to be removed to make more room for His presence. God didn't just give me kindness and gentleness, love and patience, He gave me Himself with His limitless supply of all that I needed. His own presence and Spirit were the source of those things. I was asking Him to improve me. He was offering instead to cleanse me.

In the front of my Bible are written these words by Andrew Murray:

"Oh to be emptier, lowlier
Mean,* unnoticed and unknown
And to God a vessel holier
Filled with Christ and Christ alone."[41]

This is a perfect picture of the result of allowing the Spirit of God to shine His light in our temples and reveal the clutter and trash that needs to be removed so we can be a temple "holier filled with Christ and Christ alone." It is His presence alone that produces the beauty of holiness.

The emptying is hard. It's hard to allow the Spirit of God to show us ourselves. And, if we were just left with that, this would be a discouraging and depressing chapter. But, once again, this cleansing is no different than that of the Old Testament temple. It's a means to an end—a glorious end. It's the means of obtaining the fullness of a holy God in our lives. It's making room for God and cleansing is a small price to pay for His presence and filling. He loves to replace our junk with His furnishings—His peace, His joy,

His love, and so much more. And the result is a life that reveals the beauty of God's own holiness.

*The meaning of this word as used by Andrew Murray is "lacking distinction or eminence."

Personal Refection and Prayer

How should the truth of 1 Corinthians 6:19 impact our lives? We need to understand the reality of these words. Paul was not just painting a word picture but declaring an amazing truth. Prayerfully read Psalm 51. What was David's heart's desire? What is yours?

Dear Holy God,

The reality that we are Your temple is a sobering thought. It should motivate us to make it a place where Your holy presence feels at home—a place that is cleansed so nothing hinders the beauty of Your holy presence from being evident in our lives. We are not our own. Help us to honor You with the body You have chosen as Your temple. Amen

Conclusion

"God will become to us the great ALL, and His presence
the glory and wonder of our lives." ~A.W. Tozer

I realize when we talk about the beauty of holiness, it's easy to romanticize this idea. It's easy to make this a vague ideal rather than a practical reality. God never intended this to be anything but a very real experience that would be evident in our daily lives. He asks us not just to admire it, but to acquire it.

It's also easy to see this as having more to do with Sunday than Monday through Friday—more to do with times of worship and prayer than making lunches, handling problems at work, and interacting with neighbors. Nothing could be farther from the truth.

Israel was to display the holiness of God in their daily lives—in how they conducted themselves in their private and public affairs. The holiness of God was to be evident to the nations around them as it was displayed in the ordinary days, and the ordinary interactions and life of the Israelites. The beauty of holiness is meant for everyday living—for the peanut-butter-and-jelly part of our lives.

Most of what I would do and say as I cared for my mother-in-law was not seen by anyone else but her (and she, of course, didn't remember). However, when I speak at a women's conference or retreat, my words and actions are observed by sometimes hundreds of women. What I've learned is there is no difference in God's sight between these two ministries. One is very private. One is very public. Both are opportunities for the beauty of holiness to be evident. In fact, I feel strongly the words I said to one ninety-nine-year-old woman were as important as the words I shared with many—maybe more important. The beauty of holiness is not an optional thing to be put on for public display, but a day-to-day reality that must be evident even in those moments seen only by God. I continue to pray for this to be a reality in my public and private life.

The psalmist tells us "the heavens declare the glory of God" (Psalm 19:1), and they do so in an amazing and dramatic way. The more we learn of the vastness and intricacies of the universe, the more we stand in awe of the mind and power of the One who brought them into being. But the heavens do not declare the holiness of God. It's people alone who can, and must, make known God's pure and glorious holiness. Our Creator is a holy, holy, holy God and has chosen us to make that truth known. Oh, that others might see in us beauty that comes from Him alone—the beauty of holiness.

What is the cost of this beauty? What is required of us? We find an answer to those questions in an incident that took place when my son Steven was a boy at our church camp.

Clutched in my son's little hand was all the money he had. He pressed his nose up against the glass case at the camp bookstore that displayed all sorts of treasures just for kids. He breathed a sigh of relief. It was still there—the amazing cardboard bee with a thick rubber band around the bottom. It was attached to a string and if you swung it around in the air just right, it buzzed just like a real bee. Looking up at Mr. Holmes standing behind the counter, Steven asked, "How much is that bee?" Mr. Holmes replied,

"How much do you have?" Steven opened his fist and held it up. "Nineteen cents," Mr. Holmes said. Steven held his breath. "Yep, nineteen cents," repeated Mr. Holmes, "and it just so happens that today that bee costs exactly nineteen cents." Steven could hardly believe his ears. Nineteen cents! Exactly the amount he had. In no time at all, he was the excited owner of a cardboard bumble bee that could really buzz. It had cost him everything he had, but not a penny more!

We gaze longingly at the beauty of holiness and with fear and trembling ask, "How much does it cost?" And the answer for us also is, "Everything you have, but not a penny more."

Special Thanks

*T*he passion for the message of a book usually begins in the heart of the author, but bringing that passion to print includes many other people. I suspect that often writers find their biggest struggle with words as they attempt to express their thanks to those who have helped transform a manuscript into a published book.

I am so grateful for the circumstances that led me to find that my best choice for an agent was an old friend. Thank you, Dave Fessenden, for all you did to encourage, help, and find my manuscript a home at CrossRiver Media.

There's a lot of waiting involved in getting a manuscript to a publisher, but it is so clearly God's timing that led mine to CrossRiver Media. I am grateful to be part of this amazing group who share my passion for conveying God's truth through books.

Thank you, Tami, not just for accepting my manuscript for publication, but for believing in the message of this book. Thank you, Deb, for your touch on my words that made them have more impact (and be grammatically correct) while still allowing my voice to come through. And thank you, DeeDee, for praying and cheering us all on through this process.

A special thanks to my biggest encourager who continues to believe, not only that I can write, but that I should write. Thank you, Peter. I am so blessed to share this journey with you.

Endnotes

1. C. S. Lewis, *Mere Christianity* (New York: Macmillan Co., 1966), 124.

2. Janice Holt Giles, *The Believers* (Boston, MA: Houghton Mifflin Co., 1957), 49.

3. Ravi Zacharias, *Let My People Think* (radio program)

4. A. B. Simpson, "I Want to Be Holy," *Hymns of the Christian Life* (Harrisburg: Christian Publications, Inc., 1978), #446.

5. Calvin Miller, *The Table of Inwardness* (Downers Grove, Ill: Inter-Varsity Press, 1984), 29.

6. Leona Choy, *Andrew Murray: the Authorized Biography* (CLC Publications: Fort Washington, PA, 2000), 178.

7. A. W. Tozer, *The Knowledge of the Holy* (Harrisburg, PA, Christian Publications, Inc., 1961), 38.

8. Ibid., 38.

9. W. Glyn Evans, *Daily with the King* (Chicago: Moody Press, 1979), 141.

10. Malcolm Muggeridge, *Confessions of a Twentieth-Century Pilgrim,* (San Francisco: Harper & Row Publishers, 1988), 141.

11. Lois DeHoff, "May Christ be Seen in Me," *Songs Everybody Love* (Singspiration, Inc.) #17.

12. Oswald Chambers, *My Utmost for His Highest* (Grand Rapids, Michigan: Discovery House, 1992), February 4th.

13. Nuesch Hanspeter, *Ruth and Billy Graham:the Legacy of a Couple* (Grand Rapids: Baker Books, 2014), 69.

14. Andrew Murray, *The Secret of Adoration* (Fort Washington, PA: CLC Publications, 2004), 28.

15. Andrew Murray, *The Secret of Adoration* (Fort Washington, PA: CLC Publications, 2009), Day 9.

16. David McCasland, *Oswald Chambers:Abandoned to God* (Grand Rapids: Discovery House, 1993), 261.

17. A. C. Snead, "Fully Surrendered," *Hymns of the Christian Life* (Harrisburg, PA: Christian Publications, Inc), #315.

18. Ibid.

19. Andrew Murray, *Humility* (New Kensington, PA: Whitaker House, 1982), 70.

20. Gerard Reed, *C. S. Lewis and the Bright Shadow of Holiness* (Kansas City: Beacon Hill Press, 1999), 92.

21. Corrie Ten Book, *Clippings from My Notebook* (Minneapolis: World Wide Publications, 1982), 52.

22. A. C. Snead, Op. cit.

23. A. W. Tozer, *The Pursuit of God* (Harrisburg, PA: Christian Publications, 1982), 36.

24. Andrew Bonar, *Robert Murray M'Cheyne* (East Peoria, Illinois: Versa Press, Inc., 2015), 200.

25. *The New Unger's Bible Dictionary* (Moody Press: Chicago 1988), 479.

26. *Vine's Expository Dictionary of New Testament Words* (McClean, VA: McDonald Publishing Company), 695.

27. Amy Carmichael, *The Gold Cord: The Story of a Fellowship* (Fort Washington, PA: Christian Literature Crusade, 1992), 70.

28. Albert Osborn, "Let the Beauty of Jesus be Seen in Me," *Making Melody* (St. Louis: Bible Memory Association, Inc., 1963), #119.

29. Helen Howarth Lemmel, "Turn Your Eyes Upon Jesus" *Making*

Melody (St. Louis: Bible Memory Association, Inc., 1963), #205.

30. Amy Carmichael, *Gold by Moonlight* (London: Society for Promoting Christian Knowledge, 1940), 18.

31. Larnelle Harris, "Much Too High Price," Used with permission of Larnelle Harris: www.Larnelle.com.

32. A. B. Simpson, "Not I, But Christ," *Hymns of the Christian Faith* (Harrisburg PA: Christian Publications, 1936), #416.

33. Amy Carmichael, *Edges of His Way* (Fort Washington, PA: Christian Literature Crusade 1975) 63.

34. Andrew Murray, *The Secret of Adoration* (Fort Washington, PA: CLC Publications, 2009) Foreword.

35. Stuart K. Hine, "How Great Thou Art," (Public Domain).

36. Andrew Murray, *The Secret of Adoration* (Fort Washington, PA: CLC Publications, 2009) Foreword.

37. Amy Carmichael, *If* (London: SPCK, 1951), 71.

38. Ibid.

39. Robert Coleman, ed., *One Divine Moment* (Old Tappan, NJ: Fleming H. Revell Company, 1970), 101.

40. Ibid., 28.

41. Andrew Murray, *Humility* (New Kensington, PA: Whitaker House, 1982) 112.

Chapter Beginning Quotations

Introduction: C. S. Lewis, *Letters to an American Lady* (Grand Rapids: William B. Eerdmans Publisher Co., 1967), 19.

Chapter One: Gerard Reed, *C.S. Lewis and the Bright Shadow of Holiness* (Kansas City: Beacon Hill Press, 1999), 92.

Chapter Two: A. W. Tozer, *The Knowledge of the Holy* (Harrisburg: Christian Publications, 1961), 111.

Chapter Three: Jeff Bridges, *The Pursuit of Holiness* (Colorado Springs: NavPress, 1986), 72.

Chapter Four: Amy Carmichael, *Gold by Moonlight* (London: Society for Promoting Christian Knowledge, 1940), 58.

Chapter Five: Andrew Murray, *Humility* (New Kensington, PA: Whitaker House, 1982), 70.

Chapter Six: David McCasland, *Oswald Chambers: Abandoned to God* (Grand Rapids: Discovery House Publishers, 1993), 261.

Chapter Seven: A. W. Tozer, *The Pursuit of God* (Camp Hill, PA: Christian Publications, 1982), 36.

Chapter Eight: Andrew Murray, *The Praying Heart* (Bloomington, MN: Garborg's Heart 'N Home, Inc., 1989), April 20th.

Chapter Nine: Amy Carmichael, *Edges of His Way* (Fort Washington, PA: Christian Literature Crusade, 1975), 63

Chapter Ten: Richard Foster, *Celebration of Discipline* (London: Hodder and Stoughton, 1980), 148.

Chapter Eleven: David Jeremiah, *My Heart's Desire* (Nashville: Thomas Nelson, 2002), 36.

Conclusion: A. W. Tozer, *The Pursuit of God* (Camp Hill, PA: Christian Publications, 1982), 59.

About the Author

One of seven children raised in a parsonage, Esther first saw the beauty of holiness displayed in the life of her parents. What they taught, they lived, and the impact of that set the course for her life and writing.

Esther has been involved in ministry for over thirty years and active in women's ministries both in the local church and on denominational levels. She is a frequent speaker at women's retreats and conferences. She has also been privileged to speak overseas in Africa and South America when visiting missionaries.

Esther presently serves as Director of Women's Ministry and Prayer at Community Bible Church in Mansfield, Ohio. She continues to be involved in the lives of women through speaking engagements, personal counseling, and Bible studies.

Esther was a contributing author to *Inspired by Tozer*, published by Regal in 2011. Other contributing authors included Randy Alcorn, Chuck Swindoll, Cecil Murphey, and Bruce Wilkinson. In 2013, her book *The Sweet Side of Suffering* was published by Discovery House Publishers. A Bible study guide for *The Sweet Side of Suffering* is available as a free PDF download at Esther's blog, ViewFromTheSparrowsNest.com.

You can also connect with Esther on Facebook at Facebook.com/M.EstherLovejoy.

Abba's
ANSWERS

50 Stories of God's Answers to Prayer

Discover more great books at CrossRiverMedia.com

THE GRACE IMPACT

The promise of grace pulses throughout Scripture, showing a loving heavenly Father lavishing His grace on us through His Son. In *The Grace Impact,* author Nancy Kay Grace gives us a closer glimpse at God's character. His grace covers every detail of life, not just the good things, but the difficult, sad, and complicated things. That knowledge can give us the ability to walk confidently through life knowing God is with us every step of the way.

UNBEATEN

Difficult times often leave Christians searching the Bible for answers to difficult questions—Does God hear me when I pray? Why isn't He doing anything? As author Lindsey Bell searched the Bible for answers, her studies led her through the stories of biblical figures, big and small. She discoverd that while life brings trials, faith brings victory. And when we rely on God to get us through, we can emerge *Unbeaten.*

UNSHAKABLE FAITH

Are you struggling to believe God's promises? Do you have a tough time understanding the Bible's true meaning? Discover the essential Bible study that will draw you closer to Christ every day. Deepen your relationship with Jesus and become forever grounded in biblical truth with this seven-week study perfect for self-guided learning or group sessions. A leaders guide is also available.

If you enjoyed this book, will you consider sharing it with others?

- Mention the book on Facebook, Tweitter, Pinterest, or your blog.
- Recommend this book to your small group, book club, and workplace.
- Head over to Facebook.com/CrossRiverMedia, "Like" the page and post a comment as to what you enjoyed the most.
- Write a review on Amazon.com, BN.com, or Goodreads.com.
- To learn about our latest releases, subscribe to our newsletter at CrossRiverMedia.com.

JOIN CROSSRIVER ONLINE...

CrossRiverMedia.com

Facebook.com/CrossRiverMedia

Twitter.com/CrossRiverMedia

Pinterest.com/CrossRiverMedia

Instagram.com/CrossRiverMedia

Growing in Christ

... from the ground up.

Available in bookstores and from online retailers.

CrossRiver Media
www.crossrivermedia.com

Made in the USA
Middletown, DE
13 February 2021

33691394R00070